Social Emotional Learning One Day at a Time:

Daily Reflections

SEL 365 Days a Year

Thom Stecher

Printed in the United States of America
First Edition

For information about special discounts for bulk purchases, please contact the publisher at thom@thomstecher.com

ISBN: 9798321321003 (print)

Cover Design by Katie McLaughlin

Library of Congress Control Number: 002417406

Thom Stecher and Associates
8 Fawn Circle, Malvern, PA 19355
www.thomstecher.com

Dedication

This book is dedicated to all the educators who give their love, knowledge, preparation, and structure to their students every day.

Teachers are the life blood of this world. From our earliest times as human beings, someone had to teach someone else so we would grow and prosper as a human family.

Gratitude

I am very grateful to Taylor Hicks for her structure, design and editing of this book. I am grateful to my sister, JoAnn Tier, for her care-full editing.

I am grateful daily to Abby Morgan for her constant guidance, structure, and counsel. Abby is one of the few people who tells me no, and I listen. I am grateful to Katie McLaughlin for her creation of the beautiful cover for this book. It brings my core values to life through colors and flowers that hold special meaning to me.

I am forever grateful for the silent, inspiration of our angelic daughter, Ashley. For 39 years, Ashley has brought unconditional love into every day of my life. She continues to bless us in spirit.

My greatest gratitude always goes to Sandra, my beloved wife of 45 years. You, my love, are the model of all the good in my life and every positive message in this book. I am humbled by your dedication and love.

Introduction

I have always been a reader and a writer. My mom, my kindergarten teacher, taught me the love of reading. I have always loved the adventure of story.

I revisit my favorite books and authors often and many are quoted and referenced in the following pages. I underline, highlight, and add sticky flags to pages so I can easily turn to them. Each time I reread; I am brought deeper into the process of self-discovery and self-awareness. Every story, every piece of research, and every dialogue invites me into more meaningful relationships. I opened to a new and more vibrant social awareness. I explore my growth as a decision-maker, and I end every day in gratitude.

You will read many references to God in this book. That is my choice. I was raised in that language, and I am most comfortable with that terminology. I also honor and respect other words and concepts used in other cultures and faiths. I never argue about unconditional love.

Every Sunday since 2013, I have shared my hopes, stories, and love in blog posts. The following 365 days is a collection of these writings organized by the five competencies of Social Emotional Learning and ending the year with Gratitude.

January and February - Self-Awareness
March and April - Self-Management
May and June - Social Awareness
July and August - Relationship Skills
September and October - Responsible Decision-Making
November and December - Gratitude

Please allow yourself to deliberately focus on one day at a time. Each day includes a "call to action". I hope these 365 days will revitalize and heal your heart and soul. Just maybe this book becomes one of your favorites and you revisit it often.

Self-Awareness

January and February

Self-awareness is the ability to identify how we are feeling at any given moment. Self-awareness allows us to connect our feelings to our thoughts and values. Honesty and integrity have always been two of the most important values in my life. The more self-aware we are, the better we can develop our sense of purpose, identity, and developmental assets, examine our prejudices, and heal our authentic voice.

January

"We are not human beings having a spiritual experience, we are spiritual beings having a human experience."
~ Teilhard de Chardin

What Makes You Come Alive?

January 1st

"Do not ask what the world needs. Ask what makes you come alive and go do it. Because what the world needs is people who have come alive."
- Howard Thurman

I am inspired by this writing. It encourages us to follow our bliss; to do what we love.

When we do what we love, we come alive.

When we do what we love, we give the world what it needs.

- What currently makes you come alive as an educational leader?
- What do you love doing that fills you with joy?

Purpose

January 2nd

One of the great joys of my life is helping others find and practice their sense of purpose. I believe that one of the primary reasons for our lives is to find and practice our sense of purpose. Our sense of purpose is unique to each of us. We are blessed when we share our purpose with others. There is no greater joy than to be on purpose.

If you have a sense of purpose, be grateful and practice. If you are not sure of your purpose, reflect on the moments in your life when you have felt joy. I find that our sense of purpose is difficult to find when we are self-absorbed. When we are being of service to someone else or something greater than us, our purpose is often revealed.

Over the course of my life, I have often reflected and worked on my sense of purpose. My purpose statement found me in my early days while reading *A Course of Miracles*, by Helen Schucman and William Thetford:

I am here only to be truly helpful.

- As you focus on self-awareness what is your current sense of purpose?
- Why are you here?

Why We Teach

January 3rd

We teach so that we can change the world. Each child who we influence is another ripple in the human change process.

Teaching and learning are indispensable. Teachers and learners are indispensable.

The world changes as teachers and students evolve and grow. The world changes as teaching and learning evolves and grows.

The world does not change because of tests or test scores. There are no final exams in life. There are no standardized tests in life.

We heal hearts. We educate minds. We empower dreams. We change the world.

- How are you currently healing hearts, educating minds, empowering dreams, and changing the world?

Neuroscience Supports Social Emotional Learning

January 4th

Richard Davidson, a neuroscientist, has integrated neuroimaging research into a theory of the happy brain. Davidson explains that there are 4 independent brain circuits that influence our lasting happiness:

- The first circuit is "our ability to maintain positive states." Spiritual teachers like the Dalai Lama and Archbishop Desmond Tutu say that love and compassion is the way to happiness.
- The second circuit is responsible for "our ability to recover from negative states." This supports the work of resiliency which is flourishing in our school programming.
- The third circuit is "our ability to focus and avoid mind wandering." This is mindfulness, meditation, and contemplation. Neuroscience proves that the ability to focus attention is fundamental.
- The fourth circuit is "our ability to be generous." This is wonderful and powerful that we have entire circuit in our brain devoted to generosity. We feel good when we are kind, loving, and giving. We feel good when we are treated with kindness, love, and generosity.

Neuroscience proves, as human beings, we are hardwired for compassion, resiliency, reflection, and generosity.

- Adapted from "The Book of Joy" by His Holiness the Dalai Lama and Archbishop Desmond Tutu, 2016

◆ Take a moment to reflect and notice compassion, resilience, and generosity in your day.

Sense of Purpose

January 5th

"Your purpose in life is to find your purpose and give your whole heart and soul to it."
- Buddha

I believe that living a life full of sense of purpose and meaning is connected to health and longevity.

"The evidence shows, a sense of purpose and being engaged in your day to day is indeed health protective. A significant decrease in stress and inflammatory markers is noted in people with high eudemonic well-being."
- Dr. Kelli Harding, *The Rabbit Effect: Live Longer, Happier, and Healthier with the Groundbreaking Science of Kindness*

Eudaimonia: striving for a noble, meaningful purpose.

The primary pathway to a sense of purpose and meaning is learning. I have been blessed with a lifelong passion for learning. Learning is my second favorite thing in life. My favorite thing in life is holding my wife, Sandra.

"Education is not filling of a pail, but the lighting of a fire."
- Plutarch

Make sure you are engaged in activities that you find meaningful. Develop your sense of purpose voluntarily to serve others; while learning through a variety of resources, i.e., podcasts, books, classes, and speaking and listening to other perspectives.

◆ What learning or sense of purpose are you currently engaged in?

"Soft Skills"

January 6th

People often reference Social Emotional Learning (Emotional Intelligence and Social Skills), as *soft skills*.

I find this minimizing and disrespectful. The so-called soft skills are the *Essential* skills of being a human being.

The *Essential* human skills have transformed humanity from prehistoric fight or flight beasts to the infinite possibilities of today.

The *Essential* human skills have helped us survive every war and helped negotiate every peace.

The *Essential* skills helped humanity end slavery and apartheid.

The *Essential* skills help us care for the environment and each other.

These are the skills of Jesus, Buddha, St. Francis, Ghandi, Reverend Dr. Martin Luther King Jr., and Mother Teresa.

These are the *Essential* skills of forgiveness, gratitude, kindness, connection, courage, compassion, empathy, understanding, serenity, and love.

These are the *Essential* skills needed to be fully human.

- What *Essential* skills are part of your daily practice?

Essential Education

January 7th

I have found myself asking the following 3 questions in every professional development I have facilitated in schools for the past few years. The answers that I receive consistently lift my spirit.

- What is essential to teaching and learning?
- What is your most important task as an educator?
- What is your greatest hope for your students?

The question of what is essential receives answers like respect, healthy relationships, passion, empathy, confidence, and creativity.

When I ask about their most important task, the responses mention:
"My primary task is to keep students socially and emotionally safe." "I want to inspire my students to be the best they can be."

The thousands of educators that I am blessed to speak with, say that their greatest hope for their students is to love learning, to be kind and compassionate, and to be of service to our world. Interestingly, when I ask parents the same questions, their responses are the same.

Based on my unsophisticated research; educators, parents, and students all agree. It is time to recommit to teaching the whole child. Academics must be integrated with Social Emotional Learning. We must take back the time we have wasted on standardized tests and return to letting teachers teach and learners learn.

- ♦ What is essential in your teaching and learning process?
- ♦ What is your most important task as an educator?
- ♦ What is your greatest hope for your students?

Teaching and Learning

January 8th

I have always loved reading. My mom, who was a retired kindergarten teacher, inspired me to read. She fueled my passion with numerous books. She always had the wisdom to give me books that were relevant (interesting) to me. I found comfort and connection in everything I read. Early on, I realized I was never alone. I could always find a character or a passage that I could relate to. When lonely or sad, I could open a book and be transported to a deeper learning, to a place of understanding.

I have spent 66 years of my 70 years as both a student and a teacher. I am always learning and blessed to always be teaching. My classroom has evolved. It began in a 2-story brick building in Burlington, New Jersey. Then, a high school of 2,000 other young adults, many colleges, and universities, and now, the world.

My curriculum is life and love. I am most interested in the stories of being human. I am inspired by our challenges and triumphs. I am less impressed with gaining achievement for position, power, and money. I am most impressed with achieving unity, gaining understanding and being authentic and vulnerable. My teaching is less about speaking and more about listening. Listening to the "still, small voice" in me and the story of the depth of your experience. I am most interested in your life and what you love and how we are connected in life and love. I find there is always a connection. We just need to listen.

- To whom and what do you listen?

What is Learning?

January 9th

"The current integrative research focus is based on growing recognition from various perspectives (neurological brain research, psychological research) that meaningful, sustained learning is a whole person phenomenon. Brain research shows that even young children have the capacity for complex thinking (Diamond & Hopson, 1998: Jensen, 1998). Brain research also shows that affect and cognition work synergistically, with emotion driving attention, learning, memory, and other mental activities. Research exists on the inseparability of intellect and emotion in learning (Elias, Zins et al., 1997; Lazarus, 2000)"
- Michael Theall and Jennifer R. Keup*, Building Academic Success: A Resource Guide for Enhancing Higher Education Outcomes*

Social and emotional learning has been called many things over the past forty- five years: values clarification, affective education, humanistic education, multiple intelligences, character education, and experiential learning. The missing piece of the puzzle has always been integration.

Whatever the name, social and emotional learning must be integrated with academics to be meaningful, purposeful, and achieve the results of successful, caring, knowledgeable learners.

♦ How are you integrating social emotional learning with academic content?

"We Teach Who We Are"

January 10th

I have been in the profession of education and human services for the past 50 years. The best teachers I have ever witnessed teach from their soul. Whether through lecture, dialogue, or activity, they are teachers who share their heart. Good teaching is the integration of knowing myself, knowing my students, and knowing my subject, in that order. If I do not have self-awareness, I cannot help my students find their true passion. I will be unable to integrate my content with the personal or the real world.

"Good teaching cannot be reduced to technique; good teaching comes from the identity and integrity of the teacher."
– Parker Palmer, *The Courage to Teach: Exploring the Inner Landscape of a Teacher's Life*

In every class, it is essential to build community. We need to build relationship, trust, compassion, courage, and empathy. All content must connect to the human. If we lose our connection to the human, we lose our connection to our hearts, to our integrity, to our lives.

"We are hardwired for connection."
- Dr. Brené Brown

♦ How are you building connection and community in your school?

What Schools Need

January 11th

Schools do not need more standardized tests.
Schools do not need more technology.
Schools need more servant leaders.

Schools need servant leaders who put service above ego, who can persevere through challenge and crisis, who will stay present even when it is uncomfortable. Schools need servant leaders who care about children, families, staff, and the diverse community we all live and work in. Schools need servant leaders who will not be lead down a false path of faster is better, force wins, and the thought that having a degree makes you smarter than someone else. Schools need servant leaders who will receive and celebrate the human spirit. Schools need servant leaders who will recognize that time and attention are more important than expediency and the next new trend. Schools need servant leaders who have the courage to share leadership, and empower staff, students, and parents.

Schools need servant leaders because we have lost our way as a nation.

We need servant leaders who will remember the courage it takes to intervene with hatred, violence, poverty, addiction, and mental illnesses. We have not lost our way because of lack of ideas, or technology. We have lost our way because of lack of courage. The solutions are already here. Servant leaders have the courage to be caring, compassionate, empathetic, understanding, patient, firm, clear, forgiving, and grateful.

Schools need servant leaders.

- ♦ How and where are you being most courageous as a servant leader?

True Education

January 12th

My purpose in life is to be authentic, courageous, and vulnerable to the truth of my life. I am here to follow the "still, small voice". The voice I have come to know as God. It is that spiritual place in all of us that some call soul and others call unconditional love. I am here to serve that place in you and me.

To know who we truly are, to be authentic, is knowing we are connected to the infinite. I have come to experience that being authentic requires a lifetime of courage. This courage, this love of life is like gentle rain eroding the stone walls of ego. Throughout this process I have experienced moments of enlightenment. I felt one with Divinity while in prayer in the mountains of Idaho, praying for healing for our special needs daughter, Ashley. The message I heard in my heart, head and soul was "She is not here to be healed; she is the healer, let her do her work."

From that moment on, I have shared the vulnerability of my daughter and our life together whenever I speak and teach.

I have come to believe that in education it is essential to focus on the courage, integrity, authenticity, and vulnerability we need to become fully human. All the best teachers I have known help facilitate a learning through discovery process. The learning is in the process.

The Latin root of the word education is educere.

Educere: to draw out and lead forth.

Education at its best, has always been about drawing out the best in our students. It is the passionate teacher that leads their students into a life of passion and service.

Continued...

True education has never been about shoveling more content into the minds and hearts of children. True education has never been about one test to find how much content they have accumulated. True education has always been about those who teach courageously and authentically showing spirit and passion that connects with and draws out the passion and value of their students.

This does not happen with force, manipulation, authority, prizes, or rewards.

It is through the integrity, warmth, and love of our full humanity that we teach each other to transform into spiritual beings.

- Please share your truth about education. What is education for you?

Real Presence

January 13th

The highest quality of listening demands *real presence*. The difference between intervention and co-dependence is like the difference between embracing and wallowing in life's problems.

When we wallow in our own or other's problems, we are codependent. When we embrace our own or other's problems, we are whole and healthy. To embrace a problem demands real presence. This level of presence asks us to be fully involved; being personal, invested, and subjective. Real presence is a decision to be a person of quality and to be nourishing to ourselves and others. Everything in life can be nourishing.

Everything can be a blessing. As the father of a child with severe disabilities, (Ashley cannot speak or move on her own), I understand real presence. Ashley, in her quiet and profound way, demands my real presence. I know that she hears me as I watch her slight eye movements. I know she feels better in my presence and as I touch her hand and feel her little fingers grip my thumb.

All life is sacred. As we share our presence with others, we are enhanced. Real presence saves us from mediocracy, it saves us from apathy and boredom; and it rescues us from carelessness and selfishness. It brings us meaning and hope.

- When and how can you be fully present with a student, staff member or someone in your community?

Raised in a Family

January 14th

Raised in a family of educators, I believe that education is a life-long process and that we all teach best what we most need to learn. It is therefore imperative that we teach each other. My own unique life experiences have inspired, challenged, and motivated me to specialize in the areas of self-esteem, wellness, student assistance programs and Social Emotional Learning.

As a parent of three special needs children labeled gifted, dyslexic and "developmental delayed", I have learned how to recognize, appreciate, and admire the individual talents of my own children: while addressing their special needs and gifts. My personal experiences of providing support, care and encouragement to my own children is not unlike what other parents and educators do daily.

I know that we cannot learn or succeed on our own. Therefore, I celebrate the importance of the school community in the development of each student and each parent. Through the work of Thom Stecher and Associates, I strive to refocus the educational community on what is important; each other.

To this end, I have dedicated my life to creating educationally sound, motivating, engaging leadership opportunities for students, educators and parents based upon James Comer's statement:

"There is no significant learning
without significant relationships."

Together, we can build healthy communities where we grow as instruments for positive change.

♦ How are you building significant relationships in your personal and professional life?

Art and Music

January 15th

Art and music are not luxuries; they are essential to being human.

In this challenging economic time, many schools are seriously considering cutting out art, music, and other extracurriculars due to budget constraints. We have been fooled into thinking that test scores are essential and only math and literacy lead to success in life. The arts are not entertainment. They are not something we can do without. They are essential to our humanity.

I am much more interested in sharing a world with people who have a soul (who can sing, dance, paint, write poetry and prose, sculpt, imagine, create, and dream) than I am in sharing the world with people who only know how to pass a standardized test.

- How are you supporting the arts in your life?

The Best Medicine

January 16th

Educate, enlighten, lift up, empower, encourage, magnify the positive and minimize the negative. This is the only medicine that will heal humanity.

"You are the only Bible some people will ever read."
- John MacArthur

Be a role model for what you believe.

- How are being a role model for your students?

Lessons From Finland

January 17th

Finland has become an international model for public education over the past twenty years. Once an average educational system, it now consistently ranks in the top three on the international charts. The Finnish transformation has not included standardized tests, competition for private and charter schools, or longer school days. One of their secrets to success cites Thomas Jefferson. Jefferson spoke and wrote about "equality of educational opportunity."

Pasi Sahlberg, Finland's renowned educator and author of Finnish Lessons, spoke at a lecture recently at the University of Hawaii. In January, he will be visiting Harvard's Graduate School of Education to share the way in which the Finnish system operates. The Finnish model shows that when we focus on equality, excellence follows.

In Finland, children do not receive grades until fifth grade. "Too much unhealthy competition", Sahlberg states. Collaboration is the primary focus. The same collaboration that 21st century skills, Whole Child Education, and Social Emotional Learning emphasize.

Sahlberg shares "Children should be learning because they want to learn and understand." We need to re-emphasize our ability to inspire learning. In the past ten years with the oppression of standardized tests, we have lost the ability to have a balanced curriculum. Many schools have deleted or reduced arts, music, and in some elementary schools, recess.

The United States once led the world in creativity and innovation. Standardization of tests and curriculum continues to produce low academic performance and a negative impact on creativity, innovation, and general health.

Continued...

A sampling of the Finnish research is as follows:

- Daycare is available to all.
- Schools provide comprehensive health services and nutritional lunches.
- Education is free from pre-school to university.
- Teaching is a highly respected profession. It is an intense and competitive career track. All teachers earn master's degrees.
- Schools and teachers have autonomy.

Our issues and concerns are not educational. We do not need to "fix" education. Our issues are poverty, inequality, addictions, mental health concerns, violence, and political oppression. Where there is poverty and inequality, there will always be pain. Our answers are whole child education, Social Emotional Learning, and 21st Century Skills, human teaching for human learning.

♦ What courageous actions do you need to take to support whole child education?

Finding Educational Excellence

January 18th

It is all too common to blame teachers and education for everything we perceive as wrong or difficult in our world. Most of the criticism comes from people who have never spent a full day in a classroom. Education has become our political scapegoat. We have abused the best teachers and schools with new politically driven, fear-based tests. For how long can our profession withstand the effects of assessment that are not developmentally sound? We have broken the hearts of the finest teachers in the world. Many have left the profession in tears. It is these master teachers we need to help us find our way to a healthy and successful life.

Educational excellence will not be found in a new standardized test. It will not be found in the new teacher evaluation. It will not be found in the Common Core alone.

We must stop the harassment of education. We must take the shackles of oppression from our teachers and invite them to participate in academic decision-making. Our only hope of transforming education is to challenge and care for the human heart. The transformation of education will be accomplished when we join in dialogue built on Integrity, Authenticity, and Vulnerability.

♦ How can you support the courageous leaders in your area?

A Critical Time in American Education

January 19th

We are at a critical time in American education. We are being asked to believe that nothing is real unless it is measurable. Test scores- if you can't measure it, it's not real. The over-reliance on test scores is going to destroy education. We are focusing on things (test scores) rather than human beings and relationships. We are encouraged to focus on "hard data" (which is more easily measured), rather than "soft skills" (which are more difficult to measure). If we believe that only what is measurable is more real, it is easier to disregard the soft stuff. We are spending so much time on quantitative, data-driven decisions that the quality of interpersonal relationships, sense of purpose, and character development is now a distant second in value. The reality is that "soft skills" are the hardest to develop. Maybe it is because they are so hard to develop, and measure, that we fear them and relegate them to second-class status.

Current research from the Collaborative for Academic and Social Emotional Learning shows that "soft skills" (self-awareness, self-management, social awareness, relationship skills, responsible decision-making) are the primary factors in lifetime success or failure.

Measurement is not the villain. The problem is a loss of balance between social emotional learning and academic skills. It is in the balance and integration or academics *with* social emotional learning that we will find whole, healthy, and successful learners. We cannot become so focused on tests, and quantitative data that we forget the essentials of good judgement and learning.

- What discussions need to happen to focus on balance and integration of Social Emotional Learning and curricular content?

Listening & Real Presence:
The Essence of Intervention

January 20th

In Student Assistance Training, we spend hours talking about and practicing our listening and communication skills. Time spent listening to our students is often all that needs to happen for things to improve. Listening in and of itself is an intervention. Remember intervention is a process of change over time. Listening is the primary fuel that moves the intervention process.

In our training, we focus on what it looks like: it includes proximity, open posture, eye contact, slight forward lean, sometimes a respectful touch, etc.

We also brainstorm what it feels like: warm, caring, valued, worthwhile, affirmed, respected, all very powerful emotions. This is what we bring to our students when we simply take the time to listen. Listening is a respectful, caring connection. For the "at risk," disconnected student, listening is healing. Our listening inspires hope. Listening builds meaning in lives that are lost. Listening seeks to find the truth. Listening introduces people to themselves. It is a key tool in self-awareness.

On a purely educational basis, children need communication for brain development. Children need conversations with adults. In our Student Assistance Teams, we intervene when we act as mentors, role models and listeners of children. We are all in need of slowing down. Our world is hectic and frightening for some children. When we slow down and quietly and gently listen to our students, we help the whole child develop.

♦ Who needs you to listen, now?

DaVinci and Experiential Learning

January 21st

What are our primary means of learning? The politics of education would like to keep us trapped in our outmoded limitations of words and numbers. Our human history tells us that our primary and most effective means of learning has been experiential. Leonardo DaVinci has always been one of my heroes.

His seven principals of learning are all experiential:

- Curiosity (Curiosita)- An insatiably curious approach to life and an unrelenting quest for continuous learning
- Demonstration (Dimonstrazione)- A commitment to test knowledge through experience, persistence, and willingness to learn from mistakes.
- Sensation (Sensazione)- The continual refinement of the senses, especially sight, as the means to enliven experience.
- Smoke (Sfumato)- Becoming open to the unknown. A willingness to embrace ambiguity, paradox, and uncertainty.
- Art and Science (Arte/Scienza)- Whole-Brain thinking. The development of the balance between science and art, logic, and imagination.
- The Body (Corporalita)- The cultivation of grace, ambidexterity, fitness, and poise. Balancing the body and mind.
- Connection (Connessione)- A recognition of and appreciation for the interconnectedness of all things and phenomena. Systems thinking.

Da Vinci developed his explanation in anatomy and drawing by dissecting bodies. John Dewey believed that "all genuine education comes about through experiencing it."

♦ How are you currently supporting experiential learning?

Whole Child Education

January 22nd

Whole Child Education is the answer to our current and future world problems and concerns. Our world needs whole, healthy, stable, consistent, and secure people. We need children learning with their hearts and minds. We need integrated learning. Our focus must be integrating our academic content with Social Emotional Learning. We must re-commit our purpose to the whole child. Our schools (teachers and students) are best served with a holistic, wellness model that focuses on mental, emotional, social, physical, and spiritual health.

It is from this fully integrated approach that students are engaged, motivated, and enthusiastic about their learning.

"Vocation is the place where the heart's deep gladness meets the world's deep hunger."
- Frederick Buechner, *Wishful Thinking: A Theological ABC*

When we focus on the integration of academics with Social Emotional Learning, we access the joy in our hearts and this joy addresses the needs of our world. This is the essence of service learning.

- What calls your heart to take action to support the whole child?

Reflections on Work

January 23rd

See your work as service to humanity and the world. Don't work just for money. Your work is an ever-changing process of serving the needs of others.

- Be compassionate and empathetic to all you serve. Seek to understand their needs.
- Treat your colleagues like dear friends and beloved family members. Don't just hire people; adopt them. Bring them into your heart and your home.
- Care deeply about your service. Those we serve offer us a blessing of opportunity. Our work would not exist without those we serve.
- Be clear on your values. Make sure your personal and professional values are in alignment with each other. Openly share your values with all you serve and all who work with you.
- Focus your work on integrity, courage, authenticity, and transparency. Be vulnerable and generous.
- Encourage the personal and professional growth of everyone you work with and everyone you serve. As our work grows, we share our growth and we become more productive and purposeful.
- Work on building trust every day. If you make a mistake, make a sincere apology.

♦ What about your Work is most satisfying?

Open your Heart

January 24th

"The purpose of life is a life of purpose."
- George Bernard Shaw

Follow your "still small voice." Allow yourself to be moved by what you really love. "Follow your bliss." Joseph Campbell offered this sage advice to all his students. Science has now proven that our heart sends measurable signals to the brain, which responds to this message of love.

We must open our hearts to achieve our full potential. The fullness of life is found in following our hearts desire. We must follow our passion. As we stay connected to our heart, we are connected to life.

- How are you staying connected to your heart?

We Are Connected

January 25th

Something eternal has been born in me.

I have no choice but to nurture it until it reaches its full growth and fruition.

The eternal in me feels like humility. All that I have experienced, I have made available to others through story, so that we all can grow and know we are not alone.

We are connected.

- What opportunities for connection are you making available to your students?

With my Glasses

January 26th

With my glasses, I can see with precision. I find it is more important to see with kindness. Integrity tells me I need to continue to strive to make sure my actions are both accurate and kind.

Life has shaped each of us. Our view of the world is based on our past experiences and core beliefs. We bring our feelings and emotions to every experience that touches us today. Every action we take is a statement of who we currently are and how we currently feel.

Self-reflection allows us to see how the world has shaped us. Our emotions fill us with textures and colors that move us to continue to feel and act or shut down and retreat.

The blending of integrity, vulnerability, and courage allows us to see each other from the inside.

◆ Take a few moments to reflect on your core beliefs. How do your core beliefs inform your daily purpose?

Pain: A Teacher in the Process of Growth

January 27th

"All the world is full of suffering.
It is also full of overcoming."
- Helen Keller

Essential to our spiritual nature, we have within us the ability to rise above all challenge. As human beings, we have felt pain, disappointment, loss, and grief, and all these experiences teach us how to choose in the future. What is painful today, can become an aspect of our future growth. Suffering is life reminding us we can make a change.

If a relationship is hurtful, we need to make a change. If we are not happy about going to work, it is time to look for another option. If our body or mind is in pain, it is time to adjust and get help.

Pain can be a teacher in the process of growth.

♦ What is pain currently teaching you?

Healing

January 28th

I believe in working together- all of us, different, unique, abled, disabled, sharing our life stories, being together, sharing ourselves, seeing different perspectives, understanding, and accepting. Our pain becomes a teacher. We become more sensitive, more caring, better able to listen, more compassionate and more empathetic.

Pain is challenging. There are good and bad days. There is mild, manageable, pain; then there is crippling, debilitating pain. It moves me forward. My priorities are clear. I move forward. I must do what I can, while I can. I ask for more help. I find greater discipline. I seek deeper conversations. I listen for deeper voices. I find deeper meaning.

We are all here on this blue marble, hurdling through space, trying to do the best we can with what we know.

I remember one of my dear old friends who had devoted his life to recovery. He had been abused and beaten as a child by his alcoholic father. When I asked how he was able to forgive for all the years of pain and abuse, he said, "He was doing the best he could with what he knew."

This, for me, still rings true as one of the greatest lessons in forgiveness and healing.

- Who or what calls for your forgiveness?

Affirmation

January 29th

"It's the repetition of affirmations that leads to belief. And once that belief becomes a deep conviction, things begin to happen."
- Muhammad Ali

In some mysterious way which we are not aware of, through some process which does not explicitly reveal itself, life enters us and with this life, comes an irresistible impulse to create.

We all have gifts and talents that are unique to each of us.

Affirmation, affirming our life.

Affirming our gifts and talents takes deliberate practice.

- What gift or talent calls to you for continual practice?

Dual Tendencies: Pulling Apart or Putting Together?

January 30th

"Whether we pull things apart or
put things together makes all the difference."
- Mark Nepo, *The Book of Awakening:*
Having the Life You Want by Being Present to the Life You Have

Human history provides numerous examples of pulling things apart and putting them back together. Our planet and our very lives are now challenged because of our history and current practices of pulling things apart. This nature of pulling apart comes from a desire to gain and conquer, and an overwhelming desire to win and own. The desire to put back together has its origins in reflection and humility. There are some today who want to exclude and tear apart and there are others who wish to include and sew together.

We all have these dual tendencies. Sometimes I feel the need to build and in that building process some things (some relationships), are pulled apart. More often I feel the need to unify, connect and heal. I seek to join together.

My challenge in seeking balance is to take time in reflection.

♦ Ponder, is your intention to pull apart or put back together?

Life's Journey

January 31st

Our life stories each carry truth and meaning. The story may be something Joseph Campbell re-told from 4,000 years ago or it may be our own story from childhood to adulthood. The story gains meaning with each re-telling. It becomes more accessible, more universal. It is the emotion of the telling, that brings meaning. It is the telling of the story that brings healing.

We repeat stories because with each re-telling, the meaning grows. We continue to express our heart and we grow in understanding.

With each telling of our story, we are brought deeper into our connection with our spiritual family.

With each telling of our story, we are healed at a deeper level. Our story is our truth. Our story is our life; and like our breath, it gives life.

It is life.

- ♦ With a trusted friend, share a story from your life's journey.

February

"To see the world in a grain of sand,
and hold a heaven in a wildflower,
hold infinity in the palm of your hand,
and eternity in an hour."
~ William Blake,
"Auguries of Innocence"

As Each Year Unfolds

February 1st

The longer I am alive, the more vulnerable I become. The more I experience, the more I live through, the more I risk, the more I become my authentic self.

My truth is in the joy of our common ground and in the appreciation of our diversity. Age, pain, loss, and life soften me and deepen my joy. My greatest lessons are silent, still, and often small. As each year unfolds, it is easier to cry and easier to laugh- and the distance between the two gets smaller.

"Vulnerability is the birthplace of love, belonging, joy, courage, empathy, and creativity. It is the source of hope, empathy, accountability, and authenticity."
- Dr. Brené Brown, *Daring Greatly: How the Courage to Be Vulnerable Transforms the Way We Live, Love, Parent, and Lead*

- Seek out an opportunity to be vulnerable in a trusted relationship. After this sharing, be aware of how you feel.

Be Yourself

February 2nd

"To be yourself in a world that is constantly trying to make you something else is the greatest accomplishment."
- Ralph Waldo Emerson

Be yourself, everyone else is occupied.

- How have you been authentic and real this past week?

The Gift on the Other Side

February 3rd

My life has taught me there is always a gift on the other side of grief, heartache, fear, and anxiety. Whether it was experiencing the broken trust of a deep, long-lasting friendship, the fear of being laid off after just being married, the shock of being told I had a heart attack when I felt no symptoms, the anxiety and trepidation that comes with learning my child may not survive…

It is not the illness or fear of grief that is the gift. The blessing is moving through the experience and realizing that there is a core of something indestructible deep within us. The moment we are transformed, we know that we are in the hands of Divine.

- ◆ Reflect on a challenging time in your youth. What was the gift you discovered in this difficult time?

Why Are You Here?

February 4th

"In every living thing there is an inner necessity
that outweighs all consequence."
- Mark Nepo, *The Book of Awakening:
Having the Life You Want by Being Present to the Life You Have*

What is your purpose? Why are you here? What is your inner necessity? What are you called to do? Your answer is your life.

- With a trusted friend discuss your current sense of purpose. Where do you feel called?

We Wake, We Breathe

February 5th

The Buddha taught that it was a rare blessing to be born a human being. Life offers an abundance to appreciate. We can be grateful for water, earth, heat, air, and love. We are privileged to be fully conscious. To be aware of life is a great blessing.

We are not guaranteed tomorrow. What will you do with today? What will you choose to see? What will you touch? What will you say? Who will you listen to?

Today is precious. Today you are awake. Do what you need to do now. Say what you need to say. Feel what you feel. Love now.

♦ In quiet reflection offer appreciation and gratitude for all the good in your life.

The Moment(s)

February 6th

"There were moments in life,
and he gave his life to those moments."
- Epitaph on Bill Wilson's gravestone

When I reflect on all the lessons and teachers in my life, I am humbled by the power of the moment. The here and now, awareness, everything resides in the moment. The rest is either anxiety about the future or memory.

I think back to everyone in my life who taught me how to love.

My Mom expressed sincere gratitude every time her young, innocent son brought in a gift from nature.

My Dad who stood at the outfield fence, for what seemed like hours at the time, when I was too afraid to join Little League.

My friend, Joe, who stood with me in the rain, under the highway overpass halfway between Ohio and Pennsylvania. He reminded me then; it was a night we would never forget. I did not forget.

My beautiful, loving wife, Sandra, who said "yes" on my third try, when I finally got it right.

My daughter Ashley, who cannot speak, lives fully every moment. They tell me she is "developmentally delayed." Ashley and I have shared life and death moments. The moment the doctor said, "you might want to have your sons come in and say goodbye to their sister." That was the moment I devoted the rest of my life to love.

The moment when the monitor began to beep in recognition that her life was returning- that was the moment that I devoted my life to gratitude.

Continued...

The moment in the mountains of Idaho, when I prayed for Ashley to be healed, and I heard God's still, small voice say, "she is not to be healed, she is the healer, let her do her work." That was the moment I devoted my life to sharing Ashely's story with the world.

These are the moments, that I made the decision to devote my life to service.

- With a trusted friend, share an impactful moment in your life. Consider the emotions that were felt during the sharing.

Awakening Imagination

February 7th

"Anytime we feel misunderstood, misused, neglected, suspicious, afraid, we are spending our thoughts and wasting our time. Whenever we assume the feeling of being what we want to be, we are investing."

- Neville Goddard, *Awakening Imagination*

Our self-reflection is a commitment to investing in our future. Our meditation, prayer and positive affirmations help us create a physical, mental, emotional, social, and spiritual well-being.

We are not our past. We need not limit the perspective of our future by remembering the pains of the past.

All life is change, constant change. We can choose to be a part of that change. We can choose again, and again, and again.

- ♦ What are you committed to in your growth process?

The Journey

February 8th

Discovering our identity is the greatest adventure of this life. I remember my early pioneer days searching, for a safe passage through the mountains and valleys of my life. I reflect on my lifelong friendships. Remembering when our paths crossed, and we journeyed together for a time. I am always humbled, amazed, and so grateful when I have found someone who sees the territory as I do. The greatest lesson is that we are ultimately on the same journey. We just take different roads.

- Reflect on someone you treasure. Let them know.

Great Work

February 9th

"The heart has reasons that reason doesn't know."
- Blaise Pascal, *Pensées*

One of the great joys in life is finding our sense of purpose. Satisfaction can be found in doing what you believe is great work. The greatness of our work is found in doing what we love. Great work can be found in service to others, service to nature, caring for the young, caring for the elderly, caring for those in need, tending a garden, keeping your home, contributing to our schools, religious affiliations, and communities.

Don't settle for less than your greatness. Live your life on purpose. As we commit to our sense of purpose, our life gets better and better.

- What do you believe is your great Work?

Stand in Your Truth

February 10th

Integrity means more than honesty. It literally means "the state or quality of being entire, complete, and unbroken." When we are whole, authentic, real, we are being integrous.

Our human history is abundant with role models who walked their talk. Individuals who stood in their truth- Rosa Parks, Nelson Mandela, Gandhi, and other names known only to each of us. We have all known beautiful hearts who stood in their values. Even when they were unpopular.

As we grow into our integrity, as we stand in our truth, we cannot embrace life's challenges alone. We need trusting, healthy relationships, and a loving supportive community to surround us. Finally, we need a deep belief and relationship with something greater than ourselves. I do not debate about what you call it. Whether it is God, The Divine, your true self, identity, or integrity. It is essential that we are in relationship with something greater than us.

- Who do you admire in their integrity?

Soul

February 11th

In my soul there are lines from the Bible, the Torah, and the Koran. My soul also resonates with the Bhagavad Gita, the Upanishads and the Yoga Sutra's.

My soul sings the wisdom of the saints and the blessings of nature. The vision of the indigenous people of the Americas, Africa, and Australia collaborate with the stars in the heavens.

The animals, plants, rocks, and oceans all pulse through my soul. The arts are the expression of my soul, voice and song, music, movement and dance, sculpture and pottery, painting, film, philosophy, and the written word.

My soul beams with the memory of you. Your eyes, your ears, your fingers, your toes, your beautiful hair.

My soul carries the face of everyone I have been blessed to know and all those I still will be knowing.

♦ In a conversation with a friend or loved one, share your thoughts on the meaning of *soul*.

Virtue

February 12th

Virtue- n.
goodness, ethicality, honesty (morality); excellence, quality (good)

Research by Dr. Martin Seligman of University of Pennsylvania has discovered that there are at least six virtues that are supported by every major religion and cultural tradition.

As we read Socrates, Plato, Aristotle, Buddha, Lao Tzu, Benjamin Franklin, Ghandi and Mother Theresa, we discover hundreds of virtues.

The six that Seligman has identified in his research are:

- Wisdom and Knowledge
- Courage
- Love and Humanity
- Spirituality and Transcendence
- Justice
- Temperance

The question from the research is: How do we achieve these universal virtues? The answer is in developing our core strengths of character. We can learn, develop, and acquire new strengths.

To assess your current strengths, visit: viacharacter.org to take the VIA Character Strengths Survey.

♦ How are you achieving you core virtues?

Our Role, Our Purpose, Ourselves

February 13th

Every one of us has a vocation to be someone.
We must understand that in order to fulfill this vocation,
we can only be ourselves.
- Adapted from Thomas Merton, *Thoughts in Solitude*

If you bring forth what is within you, what you bring forth will save you: if you do not bring forth what is within you, what you do not bring forth will destroy you.
- Adapted from the Gospel of Thomas

By being here you are bringing forth what is within you. I can see it in your eyes- I can see it in your hearts. Ask yourself these questions:

- Am I living fully now?
- Am I sharing everything I can share?
- Am I giving all I can give?
- Am I doing all I can do?

We feel happiest and most fulfilled when meeting the challenge of bringing our sense of purpose into the world. Fulfillment happens not by retreating from the world, but by full engagement.

"Each one of us matters, has a role to play,
and makes a difference."
- Jane Goodall

◆ Who are the people around you (family, school, neighborhood) who are living their purpose?

Broken Heart

February 14th

"God breaks the heart again and again until it stays open."
- Inayat Khan

When I was young, my first fall from love broke my heart like lightning splitting a tree.

Years later, as a young father, Ashely's diagnosis of intellectual developmental disorder broke me like a hurricane shatters glass.

Then, being diagnosed with a life-threatening heart disease broke me like a bone that breaks with a loud snap and brings you to your knees.

Recently, seeing the joyful tear-filled face of a young man broke me like warm water pounding the pain from my shoulders.

Each time, my reflex was to close-up, to recover, but the spirit had broken through.

I will never close again.

- How do you keep your heart open?

Happiness

February 15th

"Ever since happiness heard your name, it has been running through the streets trying to find you.
And several times in the last week, God himself has even come to my door, asking me for your address!"
- Hafiz

Every day is a day for giving thanks. It is an opportunity for gratitude. Expressing our gratitude paves the way for happiness. Happiness is the loving joy of God impacting our life. The innocence of happiness can be found in a toddler's infectious laughter, or from a puppy playing in the snow. Otters playing in the water, bear cubs sliding down a hill, or squirrels chasing each other from branch to branch; these are examples of innocent happiness in nature.

Laughter is great medicine. Healing chemicals are released from the brain into the body when we laugh. Serotonin and oxytocin feed the body and joy heals the soul.

"We are created by a love that couldn't contain itself,
so it spilled over into expressions of itself as us."
- Reverend Katherine Saux

◆ How are you offering thanks for the joy in your life?

Ashley's Lessons of Love

February 16th

In my house, there lives an angel. She does not speak. She does not offer prophecy or ask for followers of her light. She is not dressed in a white, flowering garment; she is often seen dressed in a pink sweatshirt and pants. She does not offer her blessing from a holy temple or church, but from a wheelchair. As she sits in her wheelchair, she emanates unconditional love. She cannot consciously move her body. She remains calm, with a beautiful expression on her face, inviting in love. She offers communication and connection to everyone who is near.

I am privileged to see her every day. I pause from the tasks of life, and she reminds me what is essential. I am always filled with joy, peace, and love in her presence. She is making her contribution to the healing of humanity. In her special way, she is transforming the world by bringing unconditional love to the people she meets and sees. What a beautiful purpose she serves in life.

I find that my life is created by the spirit in which I respond to the world. When choosing to respond to any situation, check with your heart. Do you feel peace? Does this feel meaningful? Is there joy?

Do we greet everyone with value and respect? Do we offer kindness and compassion to those in the supermarket lane? Can we retain our sense of humor in highway traffic?

I am living my life knowing that whatever good I can offer is an act of my love for life. In the end, we will not ask to have more time in the office or the work setting. We will ask for more time with those we love. Use every moment to give and receive love.

- How are giving and receiving love?

Moments

February 17th

"The best portion of a good man's life, his little, nameless, unremembered acts of kindness and love."
- William Wordsworth, "Lines Composed a Few Miles Above Tintern Abbey"

Moments. Our life and all that is meaningful is made up of moments. Moments of saying hello or good morning to strangers passing on the street. A smile to someone who looks troubled. A breath of fresh air on a cool day. Sharing a laugh with an acquaintance. Holding your loved one's hand in a grip that feels familiar. Smelling your loved one's hair and remembering. All our human moments. These are the moments I will remember when it is time to leave this life.

Let us all make more moments. Before we engage in business, let's ask about family and health. Let's give compliments to those who serve us every day. Take nothing or no one for granted.

Be aware of all moments that have touched your life. Our values and core beliefs help us create new moments. Let us all create new moments full of meaning and joy.

♦ What lessons have you learned from some of the key moments in your life?

Reflections

February 18th

"There comes a moment in every life when the universe presents you with an opportunity to rise to your potential. An open door that only requires heart to walk through, seize it and hang on. The choice is never simple. It's never easy. It's not supposed to be, but those who travel this path have always looked back and realized that the test was always about the heart. The rest is just practice."

- Jaime Buckley, *Wanted: Hero*

I believe we are here to be truly human. Vulnerable, transparent, and authentic. I pray that we all become what we were born to be, an emanation of Divine light. I pray that every day I have the courage to stay open and be fully in each moment. I want to immerse myself in the fullness of this life. I want all my compassion, empathy, and integrity to be blessings in the lives of all those I have been privileged to serve. It is my passion for humanity that brings me the greatest joy. Upon deep reflection, I believe all I've ever really taught was how to be fully human.

To be a teacher of value, I believe there needs to be full engagement in each moment. As I stand in my truth, I pray that I reflect what truly matters. I hope my light shines for others to find their path.

♦ How are you rising to your potential?

Enlightenment

February 19th

"Enlightenment for a wave is the moment the wave realizes that it is water. At that moment, all fear of death disappears."
- Thich Nhãt Hahn, *No Death, No Fear*

"Enlightenment is the moment we realize;
we are made of love."
- Mark Nepo

As I lay on the physical therapy table, just 3 feet from my fellow therapy patient I am aware that we are all more similar that we are different. We are both human, we are both in pain and we both seek healing. We put our bodies in the hands of other humans. We trust that our therapist is skilled and compassionate. Our bodies are very small boundaries from what lies inside. A moment of grace reminds me what I come from, what I am made of and ultimately where I am going.

Will you go there with me?

- Where are you growing in your life?

Gratitude

February 20th

There is no prescribed set of lessons that bring us peace and contentment. We each have our own path to discover and experience. The work of our life is to overcome our common human mistakes that are part of our inherited ego.

I have found that gratitude is an essential aspect of the work.

The challenge is to remember our true nature. We are children of God, emanations of Divinity. Every day appreciate the blessings of life. In appreciation and gratitude, we are transformed back to our true, spiritual natures. In gratitude we make a conscious choice to focus on the good, the kind, and the loving in each moment. We build the foundation of our lives on these grateful moments.

Let us pause and be mindful. Breathe and be thankful for the life we give and receive in grace.

- How are you offering gratitude today?

Rest

February 21st

The seasons come and go.

Spring brings us flowers breaking through the thawing ground.

Summer warms all life. Even the days too hot for comfort serve to grow living things.

Fall invited decline and letting go. Even when we want to hold on.

Winter invites us to rest and reflect.

- How are you giving yourself rest today?

Love, Kindness, and Forgiveness

February 22nd

"Ignorance does not yield to attack, but it dissipates in the light, and nothing dissolves dishonesty faster than the simple act of revealing the truth. The only way to enlarge one's power in the world is by increasing one's integrity, understanding and capacity for compassion."

- Dr. David Hawkins, *Power vs. Force: The Hidden Determinants of Human Behavior*

My life experience has taught me that love, kindness, and forgiveness are the only sane and satisfactory responses to ignorance, hatred, and negativity. Sharing our truth is showing the light of our spirit. I believe in and try to practice authenticity and transparency in my interactions. I try to speak my truth with love, kindness, integrity, and compassion.

- How are you speaking your truth?
- Where and to whom do you still need to speak your truth?

Go Deeper

February 23rd

"God listens not to your words save when He himself utters them through your lips."
- Kahlil Gibran, *The Prophet*

Prayer lives within our hearts. It is peaceful amidst the challenges of life. It calls you "go deeper- do more." It calls you to express yourself as a child of God. In the silence of your soul, prayer emerges into being, to celebrating the glory of God. It is called uplifting. Transforming, healing, and wholeness.

Spirit is speaking to you.
It yearns to speak through you.
Listen to it, hear it, speak it.
Surrender to it.
Be it.

- How do you hear spirit speaking to you?

Everyday Miracles

February 24th

"There are two ways to live your life.
One is as though nothing is a miracle.
The other is as though everything is a miracle."
- Albert Einstein

I live with miracles every day. I know that tears heal, courage is embracing vulnerability, forgiveness nourishes both the giver and the receiver. We have all experienced loss and pain. We all have had others ridicule and reject us. We stand up in life because we can, and we must. We love because it is our nature. We see beauty in all things because we are unafraid of being authentic. We are not alone. You are the miracle the world needs now.

◆ What actions can you take today that will make a difference in someone's life?

"The Still, Small Voice"

February 25th

"The intuitive mind is a special gift, and the rational mind is a faithful servant. We have created a society that honors the servant and forgotten the gift."
- Albert Einstein

All the good in my life has come from following the "still, small voice."

- What calls to you?
- How is your intuition beckoning you?

Surrender

February 26th

"Let me keep surrendering myself until I am utterly transparent."
- Psalm 19, *A Book of Psalms: Selected and Adapted from the Hebrew* by Stephen Mitchell

I strive to stay open, be authentic, be real. In staying open, we are choosing to be vulnerable. Dr. Brené Brown reminds us that vulnerability is the birthplace of human greatness. Spirit asks us to be receptive. By letting life in, we trust the process. Life is continually building and breaking down and we are part of this process. The challenge is staying open, renewing our trust and being transparent. I am still learning and that is the process of life.

- How are you keeping your heart and mind open?
- What causes you to close-up and self-protect?

Self-Reflection

February 27th

I love self-reflection. This humble assessment is the beginning of growth and development. When we focus internally, we find the reason we were born. Our purpose is to serve.

"The only journey is the one within."
- Rilke

"In fact, my soul and yours are the same.
You appear in me, I in you. We hide in each other."
- Rumi

"I am in my Father, and you in me, and I in you."
- John 14:20, *The Holy Bible, English Standard Version*

We walk together when we walk with God. We are all connected to Divinity. Move with reverence for all life. Build and rebuild relationships. Rejoice, every face you see is the face of God.

♦ Where do you see the sacred in others?

Enthusiasm

February 28th

The word enthusiasm has its roots in the Greek language.

'En' (one with)
'Theos' (the Divine)

So, enthusiasm literally means to be one with the Divine.

When we are enthusiastic, we are connected. We are whole. We cannot force ourselves to be enthusiastic. Enthusiasm is spontaneous. It happens when we are fully immersed in life. It happens when we are passionately one with an idea, a project, a practice, or a person. It is an experience of unity filled with joy.

- When are you most enthusiastic?

Educating the Heart

February 29th

"Educating the mind without educating the heart
is no education at all."
- Aristotle

One of the principal concepts that motivates me to still be working full-time as a teacher at 71 years of age is the truth. I love to share, reflect, and search for the truth. I find that in my authenticity and vulnerability, I find my truth and can better listen to your truth.

In my teaching I love to create a safe emotional environment where we can create community. In an emotionally safe community, the truth can be revealed, spoken and experienced When we share our truth with each other; our perspective, understanding, compassion and empathy grows. As we share the depth of our truth, we open ourselves and each other to the spiritual.

"I am a ripple in the ocean of God, and I want to be able to see my reflection in the face of everyone I meet, to understand that even people I will never know are reflections of my undisguised self."
- Mark Nepo, T*he Book of Awakening:*
Having the Life You Want by Being Present to the Life You Have

---

♦ How are you building community in your personal and professional life?

Self-Management

March and April

Managing my emotions is a skill dependent on self-awareness, we must first be able to identify how we feel before we can manage these feelings. The ability to identify and implement stress and time management strategies is a significant aspect of this competency. Self-management includes the skill of self-discipline which allows us to stick to a project and see it through to completion.

March

"The last of all human freedom is to choose one's attitude in every given set of circumstances."
~ Viktor E. Frankl,
Man's Search for Meaning

Communication, Communion, Community, and Unity

March 1st

This past week I had the privilege to work with an old friend and 70 educators on the topic of communication. The word communicate has its origin in the Latin commun, meaning "common." Ideally, when we communicate, we share our understanding of what we have in common. The word communion shares the same origin. In communion, we have a shared experience. The word community also has its roots in the Latin word commun. Community contains the word unity. Human evolution and human possibilities are reflected in each of these words.

We need to focus on what we have in common. We need to seek understanding so we can find common ground. We need to look for opportunities to experience communion. I believe these actions and intentions will lead us to building community. In this process, we will experience unity.

Our great ancestors survived because they cared for one another. We are part of great legacy of bonding together for survival. Fear used to bring us together to stay safe in our caves with our clans. Now, fear creates hate which tears us apart. There is no security in racism, sexism, bullying or harassment. Security will never be formed in separation. The only safe and sane responses to challenges of our time are Communication, Communion, Community, and Unity.

- How are you developing community in your school?

Making Mistakes

March 2nd

We all make mistakes. We have all done something that hurt someone or given our less-than-best work. This only makes us human. Our mistakes are learning opportunities. They give us a chance to learn, grow, change, improve, transform. Mistakes do not make us bad, weak, unworthy, stupid, or less than anyone else.

We must stop blaming ourselves and others for mistakes. Blame is judgment. Blame and judgment create suffering. How much do we have to suffer? How much blame is enough? How long do we need to live with blame, judgement, and suffering? How much self-punishment is enough?

We need to be gentle with ourselves. Deep reflection shows that we have punished ourselves for being human. We were naïve, innocent, and lacked information or education. We all did the best we could with what we knew and who we were in that moment.

We are all, at essence, a whole and perfect emanation of Divinity. In our humanity, we are on a journey to rediscover spiritual truth. We are not Jesus or Buddha. We have not reached enlightenment. The consequences of our mistakes help us learn and grow towards enlightenment. We become expressions of Divinity. When we make mistakes, we focus on our oneness with spirit and learn from the mistake. Take responsibility, apologize, learn, change, grow, and correct the action. Forgive yourself and others, acknowledge we are all learning.

- What actions can you make to offer yourself grace and forgiveness?

Live Your Dream

March 3rd

Every dream, every vision, every fragile secret desire of your spirit is life assuring you that you are one with your dream. Our dreams are not to be taken lightly. They are not "daydreams." They are soul dreams. They have been sent to us by God. We are part of that Divinity. When we reach for our dreams, Divinity is always there to assist.

Some ideas that I share with my students on achieving our dreams:

- Write a vision statement. Write it in the first person, present tense. This way you can feel it and sense it as if you are living it in the here and now.
- Take time to visualize your vision statement. Relax and see it in your mind's eye.
- Create a support group or team that can help you accomplish your vision. Be sure to include people who have been down the dream road you are traveling.
- Let go of negative people, places and behaviors that will roadblock your dream.
- Take baby steps. Your new business may start as a weekend or evening activity. Take a new step toward your dream, now.

As human beings, we have an innate, overwhelming, biological need to be creative. We need to contribute something of value to this life. We need to feel that we have made a difference.

"Whatever you can do or dream you can, begin it.
Boldness has genius, magic, and power in it. Begin it now."
- Goethe

◆ What one step can you take toward your dream today?

Learning the Essential Lesson

March 4th

Hearing a doctor say heart attack or cancer has a very specific way of giving our mind a pinpoint focus. I believe that social emotional learning can do the same thing. Courageously exploring authenticity, vulnerability, and integrity like a life-threatening diagnosis is a blessing.

"The unexamined life is not worth living."
- Socrates

I passionately agree with this quote as this life is an exquisite learning process. We enter the classroom of life unprepared and inadequate. Social Emotional Learning is the best preparation I have found for the challenges of life. Whole child education, balancing the mind and the heart, enables us to find our sense of purpose or mission; even in a world that breaks us repeatedly. Social Emotional Learning helps us gain perspective, resiliency, a belief in possibilities, and passion for life.

Sometimes it takes illness, knowing you have already lived longer than you will live to learn the essential lesson.

Life continues to speak to me. Be still, be courageous, listen.

- What are a few of your essential learnings?

Mr. Rogers

March 5th

"This world needs a sense of worth, and it will achieve it only by its people feeling that they are worthwhile."
- Fred Rogers

I remember watching Mr. Rogers with my children when they were young. His kind, gentle demeanor was a moment of peace in a hectic world. Mr. Rogers always seemed to find the good in everyone.

I am aware that I am sometimes harsh with self-assessment. I am learning there is great value in asking what is right with me as well as what needs to improve. A positive inventory could include the following questions:

- What are my positive character traits?
- What skills and talents do I have?
- In what ways have I been kind?
- When have I stood up for myself or others in need?
- Am I comfortable asking for help?
- Do I set healthy boundaries?
- What have I accomplished that was previously a fear?
- Am I loving in my relationships?
- Am I close to God?
- How am I changing and growing?
- Am I grateful?
- Have I forgiven myself and others?

As you are considering these, be gentle and kind towards yourself.

♦ Through dialogue, share your answers to these questions with a trusted friend.

A Life Devoted to Learning

March 6th

Our gifts come from our wounds. The gifts do not heal the wounds, but it makes sense of the wounds. They give it meaning.

Do what you know is right, even if others don't approve.

Know your purpose and do it with all your passion. Let go of the outcome. Do everything in service to God and humanity. Surrender the whole process. Surrender to the Divine, surrender to the Divine within you, and the Divine within all human beings. Your purpose is your path to your spiritual home.

Follow the still, small voice. Listen for Divine guidance. Let go of ego and self-doubt. See the Divine in every human being. See the Divine in yourself. Act from this guidance. Your actions will be authentic, courageous, and full of integrity. You will create joy for yourself and the whole world.

Gandhi devoted his life to this learning.

"He who devotes himself to service…will grasp the necessity for it and will continually grow richer in faith…if we cultivate the habit of doing service deliberately, our desire for service will grow stronger and will make not only our own happiness but that of the whole world."
- Gandhi

♦ How have your wounds helped you be of service?

Love and Kindness

March 7th

"We've learned to fly the air like birds.
We've learned to swim the seas like fish.
And yet, we haven't learned to walk the earth
as brothers and sisters."
- Reverend Dr. Martin Luther King Jr.

For many years, I have known the impact of love and kindness on our physical health. I have shared stories of this impact.

Recently, I read the following in Dr. Kelli Harding's book, *The Rabbit Effect: Live Longer, Happier, and Healthier with the Groundbreaking Science of Kindness.*

"Our physical health and well-being are intimately connected to our social and emotional health. In the 1970's, we found rabbits developed heart diseases like humans, if fed a diet high in fat. When fed diets heavy in fat, the rabbits had high cholesterol and high blood pressure. They were destined for heart attack and stroke. All were going to die because of their diet. All of them except those that were loved. One group of rabbits had significantly fewer fatty deposits in their arteries. The rabbits with healthy hearts had been touched, cuddled, petted, and talked to by their post doc lab worker. Because they were loved, they would live."

"Kindness and love make a difference in our overall health and well-being. Ultimately, what affects our health in the most meaningful ways has as much to do with how we treat one another, how we live, and how we talk about what it means to be human, than with anything that happens in the doctor's office."

Continued...

Social Emotional Learning is intimately connected to our health and wellness. It is the convergence point for health, wellness, diversity, equity, relationships, and community. Social Emotional Learning connects love and kindness to how we treat ourselves, how we treat each other, and how we treat our world.

- How are you treating yourself with love and kindness?

You Are…

March 8th

"You are braver than you believe, stronger than you seem, and smarter than you think."
- Christopher Robin to Winnie-the-Pooh, created by A.A. Milne, *Winnie-the-Pooh*

Braver…

Stronger…

Smarter…

♦ Reflect on this Christopher Robin statement and discuss its truth for you in conversation with a friend.

Vulnerability

March 9th

The research of Dr. Brené Brown points to vulnerability and authenticity as our greatest strength. Our honest flaws and our fearful secrets are often the sweetest, richest parts of our life. We are not perfect. It is where we have been broken and healed that our transformation resides.

I am aware that, at this point in my life, some relationships and dreams that have crumbled have given rise to my next dream and greatest gifts. *Every time someone has been disappointed because I was not what they wanted me to be, I have become more of what I needed to be.* Each time I have allowed my honest vulnerability, I have become more authentic.

I hope to remember with my next fall, I am getting ready to stand up again into a new and better self.

- ♦ In conversation with a trusted friend or loved one discuss one of your falls and how you rose and grew from the experience.

A Creed

March 10th

Be kind and gentle to yourself and the world is more peaceful.

Forgive yourself and others will feel your forgiveness.

Respect yourself and you will treat others with respect.

Look for the good in yourself; and you will see the good in everyone.

Be grateful.

Trust.

Accept yourself. Accept others. We are all doing the best we can, with what we know.

Optimism is a choice. Let go of negativity.

Be willing. "The willingness is all."

Say "Yes" to life. Embrace life.

◆ What creed do you live by?

Follow Your Heart

March 11th

If you are quietly in joy, if you feel fulfilled and at peace, you are on your true path. You are on purpose in this life.

If you are troubled, in conflict, anxious, or fearful something is off; pay attention. The still, small voice is speaking to you.

Your peace will come when your soul is on purpose. It is the purpose that you were born to fulfill.

Follow your truth.
Be happy now.
Be on purpose.
Share your heart.
Follow your heart.
Transformation is possible in this life.

◆ In quiet reflection, listen to your "still, small voice." What are you being called to follow?

Our Power to Soar

March 12th

We have all experienced rejection. It is painful. Being treated as if you do not exist can be equally as painful.

Today, I watched a beautiful red-tailed hawk flying overhead. The hawk did not need my approval, recognition, or acceptance. He was majestic entirely on his own.

As human beings, our greatness can seem elusive. It can seem tethered to the opinions of others. Like the red-tailed hawk, we must connect with our deeper selves and believe in our power to soar.

We must be willing to sacrifice our need for approval. God has given all of us gifts. We must be true to our gifts, with or without the approval of others.

♦ Consider the last time you felt joy, simply for the sake of feeling joy.

Choose Courage

March 13th

"Do the thing you fear most, and the death of fear is certain."
- Mark Twain

Courage is not the absence of fear. Courage is the belief that there is something else more important than fear.

To move past fear, we must be clear on our vision. When our vision is clear, we move towards it. We take action to make our dreams real. We do the foot work. We make calls, we contact friends, we create a support system. We learn, we grow, we move forward.

♦ Reflect on the last time you felt fear and moved through it. Write about the ingredients of this experience.

Fairness

March 14th

When I break a glass, or it shatters on the kitchen floor, my first reaction is to be self-critical. When someone's heart breaks, I want to fix it. When my heart breaks, I retreat to a deep, dark place for a day or two. Our human response is to think this breaking is unfair.

Life has taught me nothing is fair. I want to stop looking for fair. Stars collide, comets streak across the galaxy, worlds are born and die in an instant. In the universe, something is always letting go or being created. Like a willow tree, letting go allows us to survive. As we release, we increase.

When we hold on, often what we hold is ripped from our grasp. In the process of letting go, I have learned that love softens what initially feels like a loss.

Being at peace, in meditation and prayer, slows down the anxiety and fear.

When I look back, my letting go was the precursor of a blessing.

- Reflect on a time you let go. As you reflect, what emotions are you now aware of?

Happiness

March 15th

"Happiness is an inside job."
- William Arthur Ward

Happiness is a state of being, not a moment-by-moment experience. Happiness is the result of knowing Divinity is available. The experience and presence of God's love is always available and within us. We only need to choose to be aware of the Presence.

This choice is made by surrendering our struggle. Surrendering our fear, anxiety, and worry. Surrender our ego and its need to be in control. Surrender to the sense of joy that comes from experiencing the presence of God.

"To me, every hour of light and dark is a miracle.
Every cubic inch of space is a miracle."
- Walt Whitman, *Leaves of Grass*

♦ Look up at the night sky and focus on the stars. Be aware of what you feel after a few moments of star gazing.

Your Light

March 16th

"The master is not a master over others; but a master of him or herself. And so, welcomes others, not so he or she wants to lead them, but because together, they create an energy field that supports each unique individual in finding his or her own light."
- Lao Tzu

This has always been one of the great joys of my life. Helping to build a community where everyone thrives. I have always found great joy in helping to facilitate growth. As I help others grow, I also grow.

As I help others discover their light, my light shines as well. We are all here to shine our light. As we kindle this flame in each other, the heavens shine with the light of millions.

We are blessed as we bless others. We are all a flicker in God's flame of grace.

♦ How are you helping others find the light in themselves?

Presence

March 17th

"I believe that vulnerability- the willingness to show up and be seen with no guarantee of outcome-
is the only path to more love, belonging, and joy."
- Dr. Brené Brown, *Daring Greatly: How the Courage to Be Vulnerable Transforms the Way We Live, Love, Parent, and Lead*

Our challenge is in "showing up", being fully authentic. For me, this includes being afraid, not knowing the answer, sometimes not even knowing the questions. Being authentic, showing up, being real entails loving the process. Fully engaging in the process of life with all its insecurity.

I have always valued being fully present. Presence to me, is soul awareness. This soul awareness, this presence, involves deep levels of listening; to me, to others, to nature, to the "still, small voice."

Presence involves staying open to learning beyond my current identity, beyond my preconceptions of what is and is not, what should and what should not be. Presence involves letting go of my ego and my ego attachments. It involves letting go of control.

Being fully present invites us to participate fully in the miracle of life.

♦ When was the last time you showed up in full presence? Discuss with a friend the feelings of being fully present.

The Work

March 18th

It is not easy to stand in front of a group of people and share your heart. It is not easy to be vulnerable and share your dream, and that is what I have always done.

I am 71 years old. My life has been a life of shared joy, passion and positivity with schools, teachers, students, administrators, and parents. I have shared my dreams and passion with anyone kind enough to listen- listeners in auditoriums, lecture halls, and classrooms. I have always done my best to answer the call- in airplanes, trains, and automobiles, sometimes on a good long walk. If you asked, I was there.

I was a young man when this started. Sharing a passion more ancient than my years. I am an older man now, knowing that the "Work" still is not complete. I am renewed every day in the Work. Every face I've seen, every hand I have held, every heart I've touched is a part of me.

My message now comes from a place deep in my soul. The Work comes from a place that has known decades of life and death. The Work now comes from a place that only those courageous enough to be vulnerable and authentic understand. The Work is always about compassion, courage, empathy, connection, and service.

♦ What have you given your life to? In conversation with a trusted friend, share the ways you have given service to others.

Sincerity

March 19th

"Given Sincerity, there will be enlightenment."
- *The Doctrine of the Mean*, Ancient Chinese text

As I age, I continue to value sincerity. Upon frequent assessment, I think it is one of my strengths. I am not the smartest, certainly not the most handsome or the most talented, but at my best, I speak from the heart. I am sincere.

Sincerity asks us to be fully present. Sincerity comes from the Latin sin cere. Sin cere means "without wax."

"During the Italian Renaissance, sculptors were as plentiful as plumbers, and markets selling marble and other stones were as prevalent as hardware stores. Frequently, stone sellers would fill the cracks in flawed stones with wax and try to sell them as flawless. Thus, an honest stone seller became known as sincere-one who showed his stone without wax, crack, and all.
A sincere person, then, came to mean someone who is honest and open enough not to hide their flaws. This honest stance becomes even more important when we consider, as the priest and therapist John Malecki says, that "without vulnerability, there can be no transformation."
- Mark Nepo, T*he Book of Awakening: Having the Life You Want by Being Present to the Life You Have*

"Ring the bells that still can ring.
Forget your perfect offering.
There is a crack, a crack in everything.
That's how the light gets in."
- Leonard Cohen, "Anthem" from the album *The Future*

♦ Where in your life experience have you been cracked open so the light could come out?

You Can Do Hard Things

March 20th

Our journey through life is renewed every day. We all begin anew. We are all immigrants traveling to a new land of experience every day.

My journey has me in a new land of significant spinal pain, daily therapy, and medical intervention. I dance with fear on a regular basis. I am aware that fear minimizes my creativity and positive action. I now must move beyond fear. I am committed to move into hope and action.

I can do hard things. I have been courageous in the past and I will be courageous again. I will take action. When we avoid hardship, we lose an opportunity to strengthen and be resilient. I am aware that I do not seek out hardship, however, I am grateful for what I have learned. I have learned to be kind to myself and others. I have learned to be compassionate and empathetic. I have learned to be understanding. I am currently learning to be patient with myself and others.

I can do hard things. I am also trying to act through the pain and hardship. I can do what I can do. If I cannot sit, I can lie down and stretch. If I cannot walk, I can swim. If I cannot stand in one place, I can move slowly. I must act. I can read, write, and spell. I can listen, feel, and think. I can be a resource for others and share my life experiences. I can help others in any way possible. When my physical skills are limited, I can act with my emotional, mental, soul, and spiritual skills.

I can do hard things, and you can do hard things, too.

- Think about a time in your life when you did something you perceived was difficult. What did you learn from this accomplishment?

"If Not Now, When? If Not You, Who?"

March 21st

This ancient truth has been expressed by many different thinkers. Now, three months into recovery from spinal injury, and continuing daily physical therapy, there is a truth that burns inside of me. This truth challenges me. It will not let me rest. It demands I offer my self in all interactions. The truth reveals itself with every sharp lightning bolt of pain that travels down my leg from my spine.

The truth is this: *"do not wait for tomorrow."* Act now, speak now, live now, love now. Tomorrow is not guaranteed. I expect to live a long time. I experience daily painful reminders that today, now is all I have.

This beautiful life is not a dress rehearsal. This is the only life we get. No more putting off truth, joy, love, gratitude, forgiveness.

♦ What is one thing you have been avoiding? Discuss your fear with a trusted friend.

Mistakes

March 22nd

It is an essential part of our humanity to make mistakes. I fell prey to arrogance in 8th grade and I discovered humility and forgiveness. I suffered a severe injury in high school football and discovered poetry and public speaking. Still unsure of my emerging artist, I sustained another football injury in college, and I discovered education and psychology.

I have evolved despite myself. I have been broken many times and my mistakes have mysteriously revealed new skills.

We all grow from the light that shines through the cracks in our mistakes.

- What have you learned from the obstacles, injuries, and mistakes of your life?

Our Miracle

March 23rd

The week of March 23rd, 2016, I was blessed to experience the perfection of God's love and wisdom. On March 23rd, our dearest daughter Ashley, had eye surgery. Ashley is special needs and although she was 38 years old, she is developmentally 2 months old.

On the Sunday before the surgery, my blessings began in prayer and meditation. I experienced this deeply profound, overwhelming warmth and light clearly communicating to me that all would be well in Ashley's surgery. I consciously nurtured that feeling throughout the week. Believing in the gentle love of God, I choose only to share my experience with Sandra, my beloved wife. Our week progressed with friends and family offering their prayers and love. I continued to focus on gratitude and belief in God's love. The morning of the surgery, I could feel my trembling ego getting shaky. The expected 1 ½ hour surgery turned into 2 ½, and with Sandra nervously shaking next to me, my belief started to creak just a little. As soon as I saw her surgeon, I knew all was good. I prayed unceasingly, "Thank you God, thank you God, thank you God." As Ashley's surgeon brought us back to recovery, he gently spoke "Get on your knees tonight and thank God. This could have gone south, and it was perfect." My reply: "I thank God every night."

Ashley is our miracle. Every moment, every day. We live with miracles. Each of you is a miracle. Be aware, be grateful. Let each moment of your life be an expression of loving gratitude. Ashley can see. Today I showed her a beautiful Easter card and she looked straight at it. Miracles: there are no ordinary moments.

- In times of significant stress and challenge, where do you go for comfort and solace?

Be Your Change

March 24th

Forgiveness is the key to peace and happiness. Awake from the dream that you are mortal, fallible, sinful. Know that you are a perfect child of God. Claim your birthright, express forgiveness, and gratitude; and be one with your spiritual family. There comes a time in our spiritual evolution where we go from seeking through the darkness to being one with the power of the light.

"It takes courage to grow up and turn out to be who we really are."
- E.E. Cummings

Show your true self through acts of forgiveness and gratitude. Focus on not saying anything unkind, untrue, or unnecessary.

"Be the change you wish to see in the world."
- Ghandi

- How are you being the change you want to see in the world?

Focus on Gratitude

March 25th

"Being deeply loved by someone gives you strength, while loving someone deeply gives you courage."
- Lao Tzu

"Your talent is God's gift to you. What you do with it is your gift back to God."
- Leo Buscaglia

"Even in a life full of challenges, like living with chronic pain, there is always something to be grateful for."
- Lauren Zalewski

"The more you express gratitude for what you have, the more likely you will have more to express gratitude for."
- Zig Ziglar

"If the only prayer you said in your whole life was thank you, that would suffice."
- Meister Eckhart

"Gratitude turns what we have into enough."
- Aesop

♦ Make a list of all the people, places, and things you are thankful for.

Inspiration in Gratitude

March 26th

"As we express our gratitude, we must never forget that the highest appreciation is not to utter words but to live by them."
- John F. Kennedy

Gratitude inspires me, it fills me with positive energy. It sometimes brings me to tears. Gratitude fills me with love and grace. I try to focus on gratitude as a daily practice. I am grateful that I can write and read. I am grateful that I can move and think and feel. I am grateful that I love and that I am loved. I am grateful for the warmth of the sun, yes, even on a hot day.

The more I commit to the discipline of an attitude of gratitude, the more health and healing I feel.

Gratitude is the choice I make today.

♦ As early as possible (in the morning), spend 5 minutes reflecting on the people you are most grateful for. Find a way to tell them you are grateful.

Forgiveness

March 27th

"The weak can never forgive.
Forgiveness is an attribute of the strong."
- Gandhi

The process of forgiveness helps us conquer judgement of others. We all make mistakes. Very few of us plan to make a mistake and hurt someone. Most of our actions are unconscious or trying to fulfill a need we perceive as important in the moment. Upon deep reflection, I find that every mistake is really a neutral action until I take offense; until I am hurt. Forgiveness is not required until I make a judgement. My experience is that judgement is a heavy load to carry. In all my reading and study of forgiveness, I find it is most important to forgive the actions of others that have hurt me because forgiveness takes the burden of judgement off me.

"Forgiveness is the key to action and freedom."
- Hannah Arendt

"We never heal until we forgive."
- Nelson Mandela

"Forgiveness is not an occasional act; it is a permanent attitude."
- Reverend Dr. Martin Luther King, Jr., *Strength in Love*

"Forgiveness is the fragrance of the violet which still clings to the heel that crushed it."
- George Roemisch

The process of forgiveness means that I will no longer feel anger and resentment for past wrongs that I perceive were committed against me.

Continued...

I forgive and I still remember the lessons. I need to forgive, and I need to remember so my part in past hurts does not continue.

For my health and well-being, I need to make peace with the past. When I forgive, I feel a weight lifted from my shoulders and my spirit elevates.

Psychoneuroimmunology teaches that our thoughts influence the cells in our body. The quality of our thoughts affects our entire organism.

Empathy plays a significant role in forgiveness. If we can allow ourselves to see the world through the eyes of our offender: see and understand his life situation, suffering and intentions, it will help in the process of forgiveness.

We need to be less invested in judgement and more invested and understanding. Forgiveness helps us transform. Letting go of past hurts allows our kindness to grow. Forgiveness and kindness are not something we do; it is something we are.

- Who or what (behavior) needs your forgiveness?
- How are you practicing forgiveness in your life?

Grateful

March 28th

My primary focuses these past five years has been on forgiveness and gratitude. I find both experiences to be life changing. When I offer forgiveness to myself or others, I am transformed. A weight is lifted, and I find a lightness in my body, mind, and spirit.

I try consciously to offer gratitude through every day. I express my gratitude to my loving wife, Sandra. She always has a bottle of water ready for me before I leave the house. I am grateful to be able to work and service schools, teachers, and children. This service brings me such joy. I am grateful for all the wonderful colleagues who participate in this transformational work. I am grateful to God for my life. I get to love, learn, make mistakes, say "I am sorry", forgive and be forgiven.

I am grateful.

- For whom and what are you grateful for in your life?

Claim Your Worth

March 29th

You are unique in all the world. You are the only you that will ever be in this life. Your calling is to be you, your authentic self. Your inner self, your greater self, your spirit is calling you to your authenticity. The world needs you. The world needs your greatness. Your identity, your self, is much bigger than your ego. You are a part of the infinite universe. As Marianne Williamson said, "You're playing small does not serve the world."

Let go of the small needs of your ego and be aware of your place in the greatness of the universe.

When your authentic self shines forth, you are one with Divinity. You are one with infinite kindness, love, patience, creativity, empathy, joy, and compassion. You have great value in this life. Move forward into your greatness. Claim your worth.

- Make a list of ten of your most significant character traits.

Energy in Motion

March 30th

"Emotion is energy in motion."
- Peter McWilliams, *Life 101: Everything We Wish We Had Learned About Life in School—But Didn't*

Fear is the energy to do your best in a new situation.

Guilt is self-directed anger; it is the potential energy for self-directed change.

Unworthiness keeps us on track; it is better termed "humility."

Hurt feelings remind us how much we care.

Anger is energy for change.

- ♦ What emotion are you currently feeling that has the potential for a growth experience?

Nurturing Your Life

March 31st

I am working consistently to be authentic, courageous, and vulnerable. I am finding situations that demand my integrity, forgiveness, and gratitude. I still work on breaking old patterns of approval- seeking, especially with old friends. I still have not mastered patience. I am still seeking to be kind and loving even as I establish boundaries for how others will interact with me.

I must be fully myself. If I am not authentic, courageous, and vulnerable, my growth is short circuited, and I feel the pain of stagnation.

I find myself at another growing edge, a new threshold. I must commit to growth, even when it is uncomfortable.

- How are you nurturing the unfolding story of your life?

April

"What lies behind us and what lies before us are tiny matters compared to what lies within us."
~ Ralph Waldo Emerson

Be Compassionate

April 1st

On a Sunday morning, back in 2016, I found myself in physical and emotional pain. I was no longer able to listen to any more political commercials. Even still, whenever a soundbite comes on the TV or radio, I find my body and mind recoil in pain. I now mute every commercial. Nothing I am hearing is in alignment with my values. I don't like complaining, so I opted for prayer and meditation instead.

My choice is to be compassionate, to understand, to find a way with God's grace to be forgiving. My value system, my "still, small voice" directs me to be unconditionally loving towards all life in all its "distressing disguises." These words move me to action. I look forward to service and giving of respect to everyone I interact with. I practice consideration, patience, and understanding.

I trust in God's love, mercy, and wisdom. I place my faith and love in God. My responsibility is not to change the negative but to focus on the positive. Today, I consciously offer the world kindness, forgiveness, gratitude, and compassion.

God bless the whole world.

No exceptions.

- How can you be compassionate today?

In the Depths

April 2nd

In the depths of honesty and vulnerability, I want to say to everyone I see, "let us show love and respect to each other."

Sadly, we never say this out loud. If we did, someone would probably run away in fear. We try our best to say, "I love you", without words, in socially appropriate ways. I love you is translated as…

"Have a nice day."
"Good to see you."
"Good morning"

"We are hard wired for connection", says Dr. Brené Brown, and yet we go to such great effort to keep our desire for love and connection hidden.

So, let me say here, what we all need to hear "I love you."

♦ Look in the mirror and say, "I love you." Linger with the person in the mirror and say "I love you" in return.

Mantra

April 3rd

Be kind to all life.

Respect the sacredness of all that exists.

Show compassion.

Be willing to forgive.

Seek understanding.

Surrender your perceptions.

What is essential?

- Reflect on a mantra you live by or may consider living by.

Intention

April 4th

Our intention is a significant part of the value of our actions. I find that the educators that I am blessed to interact with are dedicated to service. The service is an intention and action of love. They seek to uplift the lives of all those they teach, counsel and mentor.

The world sees excellence as dedication to the highest standards. The educators I am blessed to work with are dedicated to the standards of respect, responsibility, authenticity, integrity, passion, commitment, compassion, empathy, vulnerability, service leadership and healthy relationships.

Every action we take within these standards brings grace into our lives and the lives of all those we serve.

♦ What actions are we taking to ensure the social and emotional standards of respect, integrity, compassion, and empathy?

Feel the Fear...Continue Living

April 5th

Fear is an unwanted companion.

At every moment of my experience with pain, fear is there teaching both lies and truth. I never want to lose my life and more intimately, I never want those I dearly love to leave this life. I cannot imagine life without my beloved Sandra; and the world would hold so much less pure love without my angelic Ashley.

As I face my fear, I have learned that in my most vulnerable moments, I am my most authentic.

When in the presence of pain or stress, it is easy to see everything as an opponent to be battled. Sometimes we see the light in the form of the cleaning woman entering your daughter's Intensive Care room with a yellow flower in her hair and a sunny greeting in her voice. It is then we know, in every instance, we have choice. See the pain, see the stress, or see the blessing and feel the grace.

We must face the fear and move forward, even as we tremble. We must feel this moment and know that this is only one moment in a great universe of truth- the truth that is filling us, moving us forward, infusing us with courage, so that we can stand in the light of a greater, more loving truth.

♦ When we feel the fear and continue to live, what is on the other side of fear?

What is Necessary?

April 6th

"Start by doing what's necessary; then do what's possible; and suddenly you are doing the impossible."
- St. Francis of Assisi

As we prepare for our LifeSkills Conference coming this summer, we remember to focus on what is necessary for our participants. It is necessary that we create an atmosphere that ensures social and emotional safety. We must emphasize our Full Value Contract in all our interactions. What is possible is that we bring our participants to a belief in their power, their voice, their value, and unconditional love.

Once they have experienced unconditional love, nothing is impossible.

- With a trusted friend, discuss one or two of your core values that help you understand what's necessary in your life.

Your Life's Mission

April 9th

"There is a place that you are to fill that no one else can fill; something you are to do which no one else can do."
- Florence Scovel Shinn,
The Game of Life and How to Play It

We are all here on purpose. Discovering our life's mission is a great gift. You are unique in all life. You are here for a special and sacred purpose. Accept your responsibility. Step into your destiny with sincere intention and deep kindness. Be all you came here to be.

- What unique skill or talent do you bring to the world?

Perhaps You Are a Leader

April 10th

Leadership is rare because it demands so much of us. Leadership means we will be unpopular, and we will be uncomfortable.

When we speak our truth, someone will object. Someone will criticize. Someone will even create lies about you.

If you dare to lead, stand tall in your truth. This may be publicly uncomfortable and daunting. Often, the place of our discomfort and fear is the exact place we need to be standing to lead most effectively.

- Where are you uncomfortable and where is leadership opportunity?

Gratitude Can Lead to Higher Grades

April 11th

Research points to gratitude as a potential bridge between a student's academic and social well-being.

Studies show grateful youth have higher GPA's and experience positive emotions.

Gratitude can foster an increased sense of hope and a desire to give back.

Practicing gratitude at a young age promotes development of self-control and self-regulation.

Teachers who model gratitude help students think more deeply.

The following strategies are from ***Cultivating Gratitude in the Classroom*** written by Sarah McKibben, November 2013 (Volume 55, Number 11) edition of ASCD Education Update.

- **Think intentions, costs, and benefits**- Researcher Giacomo Bono suggests that when students' express gratitude, educators should encourage them to notice intentions (the thought behind the gift that they received), appreciate costs (someone went out of their way or made sacrifices to help them), and recognize the benefits (someone provided them with a gift or a kind act that has personal value).
- **Use a gratitude journal**- This may be one of the simplest ways to increase gratitude. In a 2008 study by Bono and Jeffrey Froh, middle school students who regularly wrote about what they were thankful for reported greater optimism and a more positive outlook on their school experience.
- **Lead gratitude activities-** Have students write a thank you letter to someone in their lives, participate in gratitude circles, or contribute to a gratitude wall or bulletin board.

Continued...

- **Pair students to increase cooperation-** Gratitude can emerge organically in mixed-ability grouping that allows students to complement one another's strengths.
- **Use question prompts-** For example, when students come into school on Monday mornings, ask them what their favorite part of the weekend was, says Bono. Then, follow up with, *did someone help make that happen?* Or, if they faced a particular challenge, ask, *did someone help you overcome it?* Bono explains, "It's easy in the day-to-day conversations that you have with a child to talk about the people who were responsible (for a positive event)."
- **Encourage service learning-** Service learning gives students an opportunity to experience and reflect on the struggles of others. Each discipline poses opportunities for service learning.
- **Model it!** - The key to cultivating gratitude in your classroom is to make it part of your own routine. By modeling gratitude, you encourage students to do the same, and, according to the Greater Good Science Center, teachers who practice gratitude "feel more satisfied and accomplished, and less emotionally exhausted, possibly reducing teacher burnout."

When we are grateful, we are transformed. We value ourselves and others more and our relationships are strengthened.

◆ How are you helping others express their gratitude?

Repeating Patterns

April 12th

I continue to learn the humility of accepting my life and my imperfections. I find myself repeating patterns of feeling sad because I did not speak my truth. Repetition like a wave breaks regularly on the shoreline of my heart. I seek to be kind, gentle, and considerate. I am silent so I do not cause pain for others. I feel the pain of my silence.

The sun repeats its blessed warmth and I continue to learn. No matter how many times I need to learn this lesson, like the sun, it will repeat. I accept my sadness as often as is needed until I learn how to break my old patterns and become whole.

- What old patterns need to break in your life? With a friend or loved one, discuss one old negative pattern that you would like to break.

Holding On and Letting Go

April 13th

If I hold on tightly to one thing, I cannot be open to anything else. I must risk letting go to build something new or to touch someone I love.

I must let go of old hurts, for as long as I hold on to my history of pain, I cannot embrace the love that is in front of me.

I must open my heart to be filled with new love.

Courage of the heart brings peace of mind.

◆ Discuss with a friend or loved one a time in your life when you opened your heart and were filled with love.

"Joy List"

April 14th

The following list of people, places and things bring me a feeling of joy and well-being. They connect me with the universe and my Higher Power's unconditional love.

- **Nature uplifts me.** I feel a part of the universe. I feel nurtured (natured). Nature exposes my child/animal.
- **Play humors me.** I suffer from terminal seriousness, so a daily dose of play and laughter is essential. Laughter is the shortest distance between two people.
- **Values guide me.** As long as human beings teach, human beings will teach values. As a parent and educator, I never stopped my values-oriented education. My children and I continue to need daily guidance.
- **Commitments define me.** They help me make choices and set priorities. They let me know what I believe in and what is important to me. They let me know where I can make a difference.
- **Simplicity focuses me.** Daily. No focus-no energy. KISS-Keep It Simple, Sweetheart.
- **Memories touch me.** They are my emotional treasures. They help me on my mini-vacations and give me my daily touchstones.
- **Miracles inspire me.** The miracle of unconditional love. The miracle of physical and emotional healing. The miracle of forgiveness. Forgiving you, and the greatest miracle, forgiving myself.
- **Pain instructs me.** I know it is a strange thing to be on a "joy" list, but it helps me learn what to let go of. Letting go is joy.
- **Death purifies me.** Another strange one. The purification process brings joy. The beautiful melting (tears). "The soul afraid of dying, never learns to live." – "The Rose," from the album *Growing Up in Hollywood* Town, written by Amanda McBroom

Continued...

- **Friendship & Love support me.** My marriage, my children, friends, Twelve Step Support Groups. The angels in physical body who floated in and out of my life.
- **God, My Higher Power, loves me.** The surrender to love and acceptance. The intimate, personal relationship with unconditional love.
- **Creativity and Art stimulates me.** Color, shape, form, texture, light, flexibility, and the process of creation. All part of intervening in this life.
- **Rituals & Tradition anchor me.** Without these, I would have no history. I would be adrift. I would not fit. I need to fit. This world needs to make sense.
- **Quiet centers me.** My meditation (listening to God) and my prayer (talking to God) slow me down. This is the time, every day, when my soul catches up with my body. Or is it the other way around?

I could go on and on.

Lao Tzu once said that the truly successful man is one who can plan to sit by the riverbank and dangle his feet in the water.

♦ Create a "joy list" of your own share it with your loved ones and your colleagues.

Inner Peace

April 15th

Our innate capacity for happiness, success, health, peace, unconditional love, and creativity are within all of us. They are not dependent on any outside circumstance or privileged skill or talent.

No single person, group, or system owns inner peace. Inner peace belongs to the human spirit by virtue of our origin.

"The kingdom of Heaven is within you. What you are seeing is not different than your very own self."
-Dr. David Hawkins

- What practice brings you peace?

Self-Acceptance

April 16th

"You each must be a lamp unto yourselves."
- Buddha

Don't blindly accept the opinion and perceptions of others. What they think or say about you is none of your concern. Shine your own light of insight and questioning; come to know your own mind and heart.

We gain self-awareness by drawing on our courage and experiences. The real you is transparent, vulnerable, and full of integrity. Be quietly and humbly aware of your best qualities.

Learn from your mistakes. Don't beat yourself up over past mistakes. When you endure a series of challenges, look to the truth and beauty of friends, loved ones, poetry, art, and music. Be still, pray, meditate. Slow down.

Knowing that we are different than others is a sign of self-acceptance and maturity.

"You have your way. I have my way. As for the right way, the correct way, and the only way- it does not exist."
- Friedrich Nietzche, *Thus Spoke Zarathustra*

- How are you allowing others to be fully themselves?

Meaningful Life

April 17th

I am blessed. I love my life. I am becoming old. At 71, I don't mentally process as quickly, and I am slower at finding my beloved vocabulary. My life is full of grace; while at the same time, I am no longer graceful. I fall down, and sometimes struggle to get back up. I get up and I rise because of the grace of God. I rise with the support of great therapists. I rise with the loving support of family and friends.

I still have some fears. I fear the passing of our daughter, Ashley. I fear when I will no longer be able to find my wife, Sandra. I know how blessed I am to be alive. Many people I know have not made it to my age. I love the viewpoint from my 70's.

I have no interest in fighting aging. Aging is a natural state of human growth and development. I actually find joy in saying "I am getting old." I am still making connections and building relationships. I am learning and I am still creating along the way. I particularly love connecting with young, passionate, caring minds. I think these relationships benefit both the young and old. My life is a blessing and a vocation. I feel called to do this work. My life continues to be meaningful.

- ♦ What meaning does the concept of aging have in your current life?

Fear and Loving

April 18th

I am aware there are two distinctly different sides of my being. There is the fearful side, that moves away from what I do not understand and there is the loving and welcoming side that invites what I do not understand to come closer, so I can learn and grow.

The fearful part of me looks for safety, security, consistency, and normality. The open and loving part practices trust, kindness, compassion, and empathy. The fearful part of me requires constraints and walls, while the loving part requires connections and relationships.

I have had moments where my fear turns to anger. In this anger fueled fear, I want to protect, run, hide, and sometimes, fight. I am grateful that my life has been filled with more moments of welcoming, trust, compassion, new learning, teamwork, and community building. The interdependence is creative, innovative, and forgiving. I pray to "be the change you wish to see in the world." - Ghandi

I pray for the courage to trust when I am afraid.
I pray for the ability to listen when I don't understand.
I pray for the willingness to connect when I feel alone.
I pray for the building of bridges when I am surrounded by walls.

- With a friend or loved one, discuss the various aspects of your personality.
- When do you feel fear?
- When do you feel open and loving?

Awaken

April 19th

When I open myself to authenticity and vulnerability, something spiritual (Divine) emanates from my core. The opening is "voice." We are all spiritual beings. The greatest gift we can give is ourselves. We are all uplifted when we share our kindness and love. Our loving thoughts, words, and actions ripple out to touch all humankind. Each act of forgiveness and gratitude benefits everyone.

I feel as if this past year and a half, I have been working through obstacles in my spiritual growth. I need to be kind and gentle with myself as I seek to stop habitual responses.

All our work is spiritual. The joy is in the work itself. Step forward, one day at a time. I strive to replace disappointment with acceptance, compassion, and understanding.

♦ What practices are you putting into place to enhance your spiritual growth?

Optimism: Neurologically Enhancing

April 20th

Our thoughts can change our brains in positive and negative ways. If a brain scan was done on your brain, you could see that every thought stimulates different areas of the brain. Positive thoughts suppress regions of the brain that create negative feelings. Negative thoughts disrupt normal brain functioning. This causes anxiety, stress, depression, and disease. The neurological evidence is clear; optimism enhances brain health and function.

If you want to experiment, think of your fears and worries. Notice how you feel. Now think about your success, your core values and all the people you love. You will notice that your feelings change in your body and mind.

Neurological changes are taking place, just based on the power of your thoughts. Our thoughts give our lives meaning and purpose.

Stay focused on thoughts and feelings that give you hope and faith. Self-reflection and social awareness with kindness will grow new connections in your brain. Inner peace and compassion slow the aging process.

- Adapted from *Words Can Change Your Brain: 12 Conversation Strategies to Build Trust, Resolve Conflict, and Increase Intimacy* by Dr. Andrew Newberg and Mark Waldman

---

♦ Take a moment for self-reflection. Notice how you feel emotionally and physically when you focus on your fears. Then, continue to reflect, but focus on your joys, loves, and core values. How do you feel?

Risk the Inner Journey

April 21st

"You are that which you are seeking."
- Saint Francis

We must look inward. Self-reflection is the road to self-awareness.

When we are lonely, serving another helps us connect. In service, we are never alone.

When we are confused, we can become quiet and listen to the "still, small voice" that brings clarity of purpose.

When we want respect, we only need to offer respect to all those with whom we interact with daily.

We must be the behavior we wish to see in others. We do not need to be self-confident or assured; we only need to practice. We only need to risk the inner journey.

- How are you practicing respect with others?

Commitment

April 22nd

Love and commitment have always been my two highest core values. When I make a commitment, it is a promise that originated in love. When I see a need, I fill it, or I find other resources that can do the job better than I can.

Throughout my almost 50 years in professional service to education, I have made countless commitments. My commitments often seem to be involuntary. I don't think, I automatically say yes. Sometimes that has been problematic. I find that more often, my service to schools, teachers, students, and parents is part of my identity. My commitments make me part of any organization I am serving. My commitments are relationships built on empathy, compassion, and trust.

I love my Work. I love those whom I serve. Together, we build a structure for students and staff to thrive, learn, and be healthy. My commitments are my identity. They are how I get acquainted with those I serve. My commitments make my pulse beat. They make my eyes shine, and they make my face glow.

My commitments coincide with my sense of purpose. They are why I am here. They give me, and my life, a sense of meaning. My commitments have brought me freedom from fear, addictions, depression, and narcissism. My commitments have built my character. My commitments have helped me answer the essential question: "What is life asking of me?"

- What has called to you?
- What has uplifted your heart and soul? Commit your life to those answers.

Love Out Loud

April 23rd

"Love people out loud. Even if you don't think it needs to be said. Tell them. Often."
- Nanea Hoffman

We are being looked after and loved unconditionally every moment of every day.

Let those you love know how much you love and appreciate them.

Let them know that their love has been a ray of light in your life.

- Love out loud today. Shine your light, be aware, and appreciate the light in others.

Joy, Enthusiasm, and Love

April 24th

Despite all the challenges of the past two years, it is imperative that we still find enthusiasm, joy, and love in our life's journey. Feeling joy, enthusiasm, and love is our God-given inheritance.

When the pandemic first began and there was a shortage of essential home products, I received a call asking if my family needed anything. My wife asked for toilet paper. The next day, a mountain of toilet paper was at my front door. The joy and love of community was at my front door.

When I returned to life after a six-hour surgery, I couldn't move, drains, tubes and wires were running in and out of my body. Sandra was there with her unconditional love. The nurses brought me to enthusiastic laughter, entertaining me with word games as I shuffled my first steps down the hallway.

If we dwell on the negative, the world can steal our joy and enthusiasm. We are each precious children of unlimited love. Our purpose is to share joy, enthusiasm, and love, and to uplift the world one person at a time.

♦ With a trusted friend, share your thoughts and feelings on a significant moment in your life when you chose to focus on the positive rather than the negative. Discuss the emotional and physical awareness when you focus on the positive.

Filtering out the Negative, Focusing on the Positive

April 25th

"...whatever things are true, whatever things are noble, whatever things are just, whatever things are pure, whatever things are lovely, whatever things are of good report...
mediate on these things."
- Philippians 4:8, *The Holy Bible, New King James Version*

We are bombarded with social media and outside messages throughout our days. We must create a filtering system in our awareness that allows the negative to pass by and focus on the positive and valuable.

I believe the above Bible verse may be a six-layer system for filtering out the negative.

- ♦ In meditation and prayer simply focus on: Is it true? Is it noble? Is it just? Is it pure? Is it loving? Is it of good report?
- ♦ If the answer is no, let it pass. If the answer is yes, allow it in your life. Your mind, body, and soul are strengthened by focusing on the positive.

Failing and Falling

April 26th

"Do not judge me by my success.
Judge me by how many times I fell down and got back up."
- Nelson Mandela

I have learned so much from my failures. I have learned more from my failures than my successes. I have learned to be resilient, kind, caring, empathetic, and compassionate. I have learned to never take anything for granted.

Like a toddler, first learning to walk. In every new endeavor, I take a few steps and fall. I get up, reassess, try again, take a few steps, and fall. Again and again, and again. And finally, I am walking.

Failing and falling is an essential part of learning. Failing does not make you a failure. Failing and falling invites you to be fully human. Every human has failed. Every artist, musician, scientist, inventor, athlete, and writer has failed. Then they continue, they experiment, they improvise, they work on their skills, and they find success.

Vulnerability. Failing and falling teaches us to be human. Every day, let us embrace our vulnerability. Let us practice falling, getting up, and being good human beings.

♦ Share with a trusted friend what you have learned from failing and falling.

Relationship with Self

April 27th

For overall health and well-being, it is essential to have a good and kind relationship with ourselves.

Kindness, acceptance, and love for ourselves is the groundwork for our love for others. We have no hope of truly loving another unless we practice kindness and self-love for ourselves. Our relationship with others reflects our relationship with ourselves.

We first must recognize our relationship with Divinity and become aware of our worthiness. As emanations of the Divine, we are worthy of love simply because we are alive. We are worthy of goodness, kindness, health, abundance, and loving supportive relationships because we are spiritual beings having a human experience.

Our outer relationships resonate with the love that blossoms in each of us. We are all worthy of loving and supportive relationships.

♦ In quiet reflection, focus on what you are currently doing that enhances or enriches your health.

Healthy Boundaries

April 28th

Others' behavior toward us is often a reflection of their relationship with themselves.

I am still, at 71 years old, learning daily about boundaries in all relationships. In healthy, supportive relationships, respect and love helps us build trust and connection. I am learning that appropriate boundaries build standards for how I will allow others to treat me.

Healthy boundaries are essential for trust and openness to grow and develop. Within these boundaries, we build a deeper connection and share what is acceptable and what is not.

I continue to find that most of my work in this area is internal. The first relationship is with myself and self-awareness leads to acceptance and love. From this self-awareness, I can extend myself by developing relationships built on mutual trust, respect, and support.

- In quiet reflection, remember a time in your life when you allowed someone to break your boundaries and be aware of that feeling.
- Also, reflect on another time in your life when you kept your boundaries firm and clear, and be aware of that feeling.

Your Path...

April 29th

The path you are on is unique to you. No one else will walk your path. We are each on a different path with different skills and gifts. Let go of the desire to gain approval from other people. You are unique in all the world. There is just one you.

Shine brightly. Others will warm themselves by your light and together you can share your journey.

♦ Be aware of one of your unique traits or qualities. How does that quality bring you joy and ripple out and impact others?

Vulnerability

April 30th

Being vulnerable is not a weakness. It is the birthplace of all human greatness. When we are vulnerable, we share the soft, gentle, pure, and authentic in us and take the risk to bring it to the world.

Vulnerability has the power to take down our defenses and crack the walls of our fear. Our willingness to be vulnerable allows us to connect with ourselves, others, and God. Humility and transparency let go of the ego's need to be in control and creates a space for the light of spirit to shine through.

"The wound is the place where light enters."
- Rumi

That place gently invites us to be fully genuine and authentic, we become real. We must do what we can to nurture our vulnerability. We can discover a gateway to a new, loving life.

- With a trusted friend, enter a conversation that explores your experiences with being vulnerable.
- What have been the challenges, and what have been the joys of being vulnerable?

Social Awareness

May and June

Social Awareness brings us into the world of others. We are entrusted in other perspectives. We see strengths and skills in others. We show concern for others knowing we are all part of a beautifully diverse global family. Social Awareness helps us understand the transcendent experiences of empathy (caring with someone) and compassion (taking action based on empathy). We are able to identify various social norms and stand up for the rights of others.

May

"Everyone and everything around you is your teacher."
~ Ken Keyes, Jr.,
Handbook to Higher Consciousness

Building Community

May 1st

I have begun reading Parker Palmer and Arthur Zajonc, *The Heart of Higher Education: A Call to Renewal."* I find much for discussion making it clear that whole child education, the renewal of human purpose and meaning must be at the heart of education. Our Work is transformational education. We invite deep dialogue, integrating the inner life with the outer life. We make real, diversity and global sensitivity, servant leadership and compassionate communities. They offer this powerful quote by Wendell Berry in their introduction.

"The thing being made in a university is humanity…what universities are mandated to make or to help to make is human beings in the fullest sense of these words-not just trained, workers or knowledgeable citizens, but responsible heirs and members of human culture…underlying the idea of a university-the bringing together, the combining into one, of all disciplines-is the idea that good work and good citizenship are inevitable byproducts of the making of a good, that is, fully developed-human being."

Parker proposes that the thread running through the nature of being, knowing, teaching, learning, and ethics is the concept and practice of building community. This is the essence of our Work. I am so grateful to be a part of a team that offers programs that explore our sense of purpose, core values, and mission. It is rewarding and meaningful to share our authenticity, creativity, innovation, and passion. I believe we can create schools that build community, mentor servant leaders, and allow educators to share their truth through deep dialogue.

- What deep dialogue needs to happen in your school to bring about true community?

Rebuilding Community

May 2nd

I am deeply concerned by the divisiveness, anger, and hatred I see in the nation that I love. My father was a patriot, serving in both the Coast Guard and as a Navy Pilot during World War II. He was also my first role model for equity and diversity as he wrote articles in support of the Civil Rights movement. I feel that what my Dad courageously stood for and spoke for is being challenged by voices of fear and hatred.

There is so much fear. Fear of those we "perceive" to be different than us. We must come to learn that we don't know someone until we know them. We need the courage to build connection, build relationship, and build community. We must stop the dehumanizing narratives that tell us that women, the poor, those with darker or lighter skin, the disabled, the old, the young and the non-gender conforming are all less than.

When we speak of "they" in derogatory terms, we undermine our collective humanity. We must focus on "we." We must rebuild community. Community contains unity. Community needs to be diverse to be healthy. A single perspective leads to destruction and death.

Community only exists when we know each other's story.

- ♦ Allow yourself to keep an open mind to a point of view that is very different than yours. Research and explore that point of view and try to find the source of the belief.

Dignity and Destiny

May 3rd

I have been reflecting on President Lyndon Johnson's speech to Congress in 1965; as beautifully written in *Leadership in Turbulent Times*, by Kearns Goodwin.

"I speak tonight for the dignity of man and the destiny of democracy. At times history and fate meet at a single time in a single place to shape a turning point in man's unending search for freedom. So, it was at Lexington and Concord. So, it was a century ago at Appomattox. So, it was last week in Selma, Alabama." He goes on to say "There is no negro problem. There is no southern problem. There is only an American problem." So, it is today with our current disrespect and hatred of anyone we perceive as different than us. "There is only the issue of human rights. The cause must be our cause…it is all of us who must overcome the crippling legacy of bigotry and injustice." Johnson went on to reflect on his time as a young teacher gaining a deep sense of purpose in working and serving poor Mexican American children. "Somehow you never forget what poverty and hatred can do when you see its scars on the hopeful face of a young child."

Close to the end of his life Johnson spoke at the LBJ Library. "The essence of government" is in ensuring "the dignity and innate integrity of life for every individual…regardless of color, creed, ancestry, sex, or age. Until we address unequal history, we cannot overcome unequal opportunity." Johnson message in the 1960's still rings true and is needed now. I am saddened that, as a nation, we still do not learn from the past. I counter my sadness with renewed responsibility to do my part. I will continue to be human. I will continue to be American.

- What sense of responsibility do you feel to learn from the past and share that learning with others?

Act

May 4th

"Nonviolence leads to the highest ethics, which is the goal of all evolution. Until we stop harming other living beings, we are still savages."
- Thomas A. Edison

"Nonviolence is the summit of bravery."
- Gandhi

Unity is our only chance of survival. Every voice, every heart, every action matters. We live in challenging times. We cannot afford to ignore or numb our emotions through passively sitting at a computer or watching a TV screen. The world will change when we change.

We must be conscious of our thoughts. Our thoughts become our words, in all our various forms of communication. Social media cannot be our only form of sharing our truth. Any action can become habitual. We must be aware of our actions and our habits. Our actions and our habits speak to our values and our beliefs. What we value and believe creates our destiny.

In my adolescence, I was aware of, influenced by, and then came to honor the civil rights movement. Early in my professional career, I was a passionate teacher in the addictions and recovery process. For the past 50 years, my Work and mission has been in whole child education and Social Emotional Learning.

Every day we must get up and act.
Act on our beliefs and values.
Act to honor all life.
Act to bring peace and love into the world.

Continued...

Engaging in conversation must go beyond Twitter, Instagram, Facebook, and your phone. We need to be in face-to-face conversations. Trust allows us to acknowledge our differences and peacefully work to resolve differences.

"The choice is not between violence and non-violence but between violence and non-existence."
- Reverend Dr. Martin Luther King Jr.

- What differences are calling for your peaceful resolution?

Ubuntu!

May 5th

In old Africa, there is an ancient custom called Ubuntu.

Ubuntu means: *"I am because you are, you are because I am..."*

One of my core beliefs is unity. We are all connected. The spiritual teachers have taught this for thousands of years. Now the scientists are teaching a similar message. In our deepest pain and our greatest joy, we are all connected. We are united. We are one. Ubuntu!

I see it in the eyes of a hungry child. I see it in the tentative smile of the child recovering from abuse. I feel it in the hug of the young person searching for identity and in the depth of those finding their voice.

It is in all teaching. Jesus said in Matthew 18:20, "*Where two or more are gathered in my name, there am I in the midst of them."* Buddha taught us compassion. Saint Francis prayed to be an instrument of peace.

Ubuntu! *I am because you are; you are because I am…*

♦ What is something you are consciously doing to create unity for staff and students?

Inclusion

May 6th

Everyone needs recognition of who they really are on the highest level. When we see the world from the perspective of our Highest Self, we radiate connection, positivity, and unconditional love. We heal the feeling of separation and exclusion.

Inclusion is not about helping people fit into a system or structure that works for everyone. Inclusion is helping to transform those same systems and structures so that everyone is a better version of humanity.

"Inclusion is about creating a better world for everyone."
- Diane Richler

◆ How are you addressing the equity and inclusion needs of your students?

Worldview

May 7th

"The world is not as it is, the world is as we see it."
- Octavio Paz

We each see the world through our own unique lens. We all may think we see the same thing, but our perceptions are all unique, complex, and colored by our life experiences. The world we see is a direct result of our perspective.

If you want to change the world, change yourself. If you want to change yourself, change your perspective.

At any moment, we can choose to see beauty, kindness, and gratitude. The world we see is reflected in our perspective and vision.

- What is your current perspective on your world?
- What is one thing that needs to change in your perspective?

When We Know Better...

May 8th

"When we know better, we do better."
- Maya Angelou

"I have the audacity to believe that peoples everywhere can have three meals a day for their bodies; education and culture for their minds, and dignity, equality and freedom for their spirits."
- Reverend Dr. Martin Luther King Jr.

We are social beings and the roots of our mental and physical health reside in our social connection and community building. It is our responsibility, as fellow human beings, to ensure that each of us has the resources to intervene with poverty, homelessness, and violence. Like the Good Samaritan, we need to be other person centered, not self-centered. We must learn to trust each other rather than live in fear of someone we "perceive" as different than us. Human evolution and history have proven that when we trust each other and learn to cooperate, we grow, succeed, and evolve. When we distrust each other, we die. Trust and cooperation are the foundation of health and humanity.

"Engaging in conversations where we feel heard and respected helps us relax, build trust, create positive connection and psychological safety."
- Dr. Kelli Harding, *The Rabbit Effect: Live Longer, Happier, and Healthier with the Groundbreaking Science of Kindness*

- How are you specifically building trust in your staff?
- What connections can you create for greater psychological safety?

Breaking Down Emotional Walls

May 9th

I continue to be impressed with the young adult's willingness and desire to have deep levels of conversation. We all want to be known and accepted.

Empathy is part of our biology. Mirror neurons in our brains confirm our biological capacity for empathy and compassion. If I hurt my finger, the same part of my brain that lights up showing pain will also light up in others who are watching me. As I ask students questions about times in their lives when they have been excluded, alone, unwelcome, or afraid, I see empathy and compassion on the faces of those who witness the experience.

There is no reality that divides us. It is our perception of reality that divides us.

Truth shared openly, connects us. Our secrets separate us. We must take time to listen to the underlying truth that connects us all.

I continually ask myself and others, what can we do to melt the hearts of those who build walls?

- What is one thing you are doing to empower student voice in your school?

Mission Critical: Knowledge and Character

May 10th

We are at a very critical time in American education. Today's educators are under oppressive pressure to have our children perform on standardized tests. Administrators, teachers, and students are feeling the pressure, burden and disconnect of "teaching to the test."

The pressure from politicians to drive up test scores is not for the benefit of children or education. We have lost our way. We have lost sight of the original goal of education. The purpose of public education was to create a knowledgeable citizen who would contribute to and serve our society. Knowledge and service. Teaching to the test may document some knowledge gained but sacrifices time needed for character development. Knowledge without character is dangerous.

Academic success must be linked with social emotional learning. Whole Child Education (character development, social emotional learning) asks us to look differently at the stresses of standardized tests and challenges us to look at the qualities of a successful school: behaviorally, socially, and of course, academically. Whole child education promotes a positive school climate that allows and encourages students and faculty to think creatively, deeply, and passionately. It promotes a team atmosphere where the success of the individual is a shared endeavor and is as important as the success of the whole.

Whole Child Education produces responsible and resourceful students who are willing and able to take on the challenges offered by their teachers, peers, and families. It also produces teachers that feel supported and empowered by their administration.

Continued...

By the nature of their populations, schools are social environments and human teaching for human learning is social and emotional. Research proves that schools are most successful when they integrate the learners' social, emotional, and academic needs.

"Satisfying the social and emotional needs of students does more that prepare them to learn. It increases their capacity for learning. Social and emotional learning has shown to increase mastery of subject material, motivation to learn, commitment to school and time devoted to schoolwork. It also improves attendance, graduation rates and prospects for constructive employment, at the same time, reducing suspensions, expulsions, and grade retention."

- Hawkins et al., *Preventing adolescent health-risk behaviors by strengthening protection during childhood*
- Malecki and Elliott, *Children's social behaviors as predictors of academic achievement: A longitudinal analysis*

We must focus on the integration of academics with social emotional learning. Knowledge without character is a head without a heart. Human history is replete with examples of great intellect causing great damage because it lacked heart.

♦ How are you integrating "heart" into your academic content?

Understanding Children Affected by Poverty

May 11th

Poverty can be viewed from a variety of viewpoints, including financial, emotional, mental, spiritual, and physical. Support systems, resources, relationships, and role models play a critical role as intervening factors. Some key beliefs about poverty are:

- Poverty is relative.
- Poverty occurs in all races.
- Economic class is a continuous line not a clear-cut distinction.
- There is a difference between generational and situational poverty.

State of America's Children 2023 by the Children's Defense Fund

1. 11 million children live in poverty, including 1 in 7 children of color, and 1 in 6 children under 5 years old.
2. The pandemic forced children already in poverty even deeper into poverty. Almost half (47%) of all children living in poverty live in *severe* or *extreme* poverty.
3. Children remain the poorest age group in America.
4. Growing up in poverty has wide-ranging, sometimes lifelong, effects on children, putting them at a much higher risk of experiencing behavioral, social, emotional, and health challenges.
5. In 2021, 9.2 million children (12.8%) lived in food-insecure households, meaning they had difficulty meeting basic food needs for adults, children, or both.
6. 1.1 million public school students were unhoused in 2021, 3 in 4 of whom were students of color.

Continued...

How do we help children affected by poverty?

- Identify the resources available to help students move from poverty to success.
- Practice a variety of intervention skills to assist students with behavioral, attendance, health, academic, social, emotional, and relationship needs.
- Learn the role that trauma plays in poverty situations.
- Learn the characteristics of generational poverty.
- Identify role models and support systems in schools.

◆ Research what interventions have proven effective to help children who live in poverty.

The Human Gap

May 12th

When Oskar Schindler was asked why he sacrificed his fortune and risked his freedom and his life to help Jewish families in Krakow, he responded, "I know the people who work for me. When you know people, you must behave toward them like human beings."

Empathy begins with knowing someone.

This coincides with Dr. Karen Osterman's research at Hofstra University. Osterman summarizes her research by saying, "The more I know about you, the less likely I am to even think of harming you."

We must close the human gap. We must become known.

- ♦ What relationship gap needs to close in your life?

More Similar Than Different

May 13th

Each of us has a unique role to play in life. Each of our unique roles is essential in building a beautiful community, family, or relationship. At the core of our uniqueness, there is a Divine seed, a spark of universal love that is in and surrounds all of us. At our core, we are the same. We are all seeds of Divinity.

Empathy teaches us that when we look past our outer shells and when we look deeply into the soul of another, we find ourselves. At the center of humanity, we all share the same fears and the same joys.

In my youth, I worked hard to be an individual. I worked to be creative and unique. I confess to being proud of my differences. Now in my 71st year, my primary goals are to build community. I strive to help all I encounter, see their similarities. I continue to be humbled to be a part of building an understanding and empathetic community.

Through years of unrelenting back pain and the fear for our special needs daughter's health challenges, I have experienced the vulnerability of my full humanity. When I was leaving IC, after being with my daughter who was in recovery from pneumonia, I caught the eye of another worried visitor in the elevator. We looked at each other, tired, worried, and unified in our grief. In that moment, I realized, we are more similar than we are different.

> "To love another person is to see the face of God."
> - Victor Hugo, *Les Misérables*

We are more alike than different.

- Allow yourself to see the sacred in every face you see today.

Uniting a School

May 14th

Unity Day asks schools to identify 100 students and 10 staff who are willing to work on the very sensitive issues of bullying, racism, sexism, alcohol and drug use, and mental health concerns. Each school we work with will select a diverse group of students from different groups within the school to break down the walls of stereotypes and labels and create a unified community.

We ask administration to select staff and students who want to address the "real" problems students face in a supportive year long process. Unity Day is much more than a one-day commitment. Staff and students must commit to ongoing support group meetings to implement the plans created at Unity Day.

The greatest problems in our schools today are staff and students who are disconnected, lonely and isolated. Throughout our Unity Day program, we build connection and encourage school bonding through genuine caring. We find that we are much more alike than we are different.

We also come to a place where we respect and celebrate our differences. Throughout the day students and staff work in large and small group settings to teach each other and address the deepest concerns in their school. We learn we are not alone. We create a unified community.

- How are you currently creating connection with staff and students?

Service is Joy

May 15th

"I slept and I dreamed that life is all joy. I woke, and I saw that life is all service. I served, and I saw that service is joy."
- Kahlil Gibran, *The Prophet*

I have learned that for me to be healthy, happy, and whole, my life must be of service. I find great joy in the giving process. I find joy in connecting people. I find joy in helping people be all they can be. The more I serve, the greater the blessings in my life. All my Work is service. All my Work is fulfilling. When I am of service, spirit moves through me. I am full of joy.

"Spread love everywhere you go, let no one ever come to you without leaving happier."
- Mother Theresa

♦ Reflect on the service you are giving to others. Allow yourself to be aware of how you feel when you reflect on a life of service.

What is the Song of Your Soul?

May 16th

Alan Cohen writes that when a woman in a certain African tribe knows she is pregnant, she goes into the wilderness with friends to pray and meditate until she hears her child's unique song. They then return to the tribe and teach the song to everyone.

When the child is born, the community sings the child's song. When the child goes to school, the community sings their song. When the child marries, they sing their song. When the child is dying, they sing their song.

The only other time the song is sung is if the child commits a crime or does something that hurts the community. The community surrounds the person and sings their songs to them.

We each have our own unique song. Our unique purpose is expressed through our gifts and talents. When we are on purpose, we are full of joy and passion. We are one with our soul- one with our song.

All our life experiences are lessons to keep us connected with our true purpose, our song. Stay true to your song. Stay true to your life's purpose. If you feel off center, sing your song. Reflect on your true nature. Do not deny your true purpose to be someone you are not. Be in harmony with others, but do not attempt to be them. We best serve others when we are offering our truth.

Be authentic, be transparent, be vulnerable, be true to yourself. *Sing your song.*

♦ What is your song? Who are the people in your community that know your song and remind you who you truly are?

Feeling the Love of Compassion

May 17th

"The Tibetan Buddhist tradition has a meditation practice called *tong-len* that asks us to breathe in the suffering of the world, to hold it in that unbreakable place of compassion and to then breathe back light."
- Mark Nepo, *The Book of Awakening: Having the Life You Want by Being Present to the Life You Have*

Compassion does not say I agree with you. Compassion says I care about you.

You are a fellow human. We share the same life.

We breathe the same air. We both feel pain and we both rejoice.

We must affirm the spirit in each of us. Compassion can heal.

Breathe in the pain of others. With each breath, feel the unity of love.

As you exhale, release the pain, and feel the light.

Feel the love of compassion.

- In reflection, identify someone who needs your compassion now.
- Practice sending them a loving, compassionate breath.

Finding Love and Acceptance in Each Other

May 18th

Everyone in this world is looking for love and acceptance. Everyone is doing the best they can with what they know. We are all stumbling through life with as much courage and integrity as we possibly can.

I continue to learn that our attitude towards our fellow humans cannot be to judge or condemn. No matter how much they have hurt me, no matter how painful their mistake, I need to remember, if they knew better, they would have done better.

"Father, forgive them, for they know not what they do."
- Jesus, Luke 23:34, *The Holy Bible, English Standard Version*

Most of my judgements or condemnations are assumptions. Whenever I am emotional and judgmental, I feel myself becoming physically and emotionally unhealthy. We cannot hold someone down in our hearts and minds without going down with them.

I find that after a period of judgement, I must discipline myself to remember the good. I must remember when I was forgiven and the grace I felt after receiving someone's open hearted forgiveness. Someone was willing to accept my faults and see the best version of me. I need to extend the same gift.

We can only find love and acceptance in each other.
We are all doing the best we can with what we know.
In everyone is the seed of Divinity.

♦ Nurture a new relationship. Spend time listening to a new friend.

Mr. Rudy Bell

May 19th

"It is not our differences that divide us. It is our inability to recognize, adapt, and celebrate those differences."
- Audre Lorde

I grew up in rural South Jersey where we grew silver queen corn, tomatoes, and asparagus. Growing up in an extended family environment, I only knew my blood relatives until I went to school. In kindergarten, my mom was the teacher. She taught love and respect to and for everyone.

I first met people from other cultures when I played little league baseball. We had baseball, play, and fun in common. My primary concern was being the best I could be and helping teammates be the best they could be. I found a common goal can bring people together.

When I was a little older, I moved to Babe Ruth Baseball. I was on a very good team that was coached by Mr. Bell. Mr. Rudy Bell was a beloved early role model in my life. Mr. Bell was a black man. He was kind, caring, and a great teacher of baseball. One day while sliding into home plate, I opened a significant, deep gash on my right leg. The scar is still prominent at the age of 71. Mr. Bell carried me to the neighborhood doctor's office. In those days, small town doctors did everything. I was a frightened kid who loved that Mr. Bell stood by my side until my parents arrived. Later, as I healed, I remember saying to my dad, "If you weren't my father, I would want Mr. Bell to be my father." The innocence and truth of youth.

Continued...

This being the early 1960's, the civil rights movement was in full bloom. People were dying for their freedom, as they still are today. My father wrote an article in our local newspaper. He wrote about Mr. Bell, how much he admired and appreciated what he had done for me, and what a role model he was for our community.

My father ended the article by writing, "If I was not my son's father, I would choose Mr. Bell to be my son's father." That was the beginning of my passion for diversity and equity. I know that acceptance, understanding, and celebration of diversity will heal our troubled nation.

We are all part of God's loving creation. We are all an essential part of our exquisite diverse humanity.

- How have you been positively impacted by cultures or ethnicities that were different than yours?

Rededicating Ourselves to the Common Good of Community

May 20th

"It is not more business that should be our goal.
It must be to bring people back to the warmth of community,
to the worth of individual effort and responsibility,
and of individuals working together as a community,
to better their lives and their children's future."
- Robert F. Kennedy

"Each of us must rededicate ourselves to serving the common good. We are a community. Our individual fates are linked; our futures intertwined. If we act in knowledge and in that spirit together, as the Bible says, "We can move mountains."
- Jimmy Carter

I admire how we come together in times of natural disasters and national threats. We are a resilient people. I experience this often. I watch as my wife has cared for our special needs daughter for the past 39 years. I admire my youngest son as he happily plows 3 of the neighbors' driveways every snowstorm. I am grateful for those who work with me and who help when I am physically challenged. We are all neighbors in this worldwide community. We are intertwined. What affects me, affects you. What comforts you, comforts me. We must rededicate ourselves to the common good of community. Kindness is reciprocal.

"We become human only in the company of other human beings. This involves both opening our hearts and giving voice to our deepest convictions."
- Paul Rogat Loeb, *The Impossible Will Take a Little While: Perseverance and Hope in Troubled Times*

- Offer a random act of kindness today.

Do No Harm

May 21st

The Hippocratic Oath that doctors agree to is “Do no harm.” Although this sounds passive, doing no harm is quite active. Doing no harm involves self-awareness, self-control, and kindness.

Doing no harm requires strength of character. We must choose to not participate in hurting anyone.

“Be kind toward anyone you meet,
because they are engaged in a big battle.”
- Philo of Alexandria

Harmlessness and kindness require that we reflect on our thoughts as well as our actions. Are our thoughts hostile to ourselves or others? Are we surrendering to anger and negativity? If we surrender to anger and negativity, we harm ourselves physically and psychologically. Our inner condition impacts relationships. Harmlessness also helps us grow spiritually. It is impossible to grow our consciousness while being negative and judgmental.

Our world and each of us needs collaboration, kindness, respect, and nonviolence.

♦ Invite someone to sit with you at lunch that usually sits somewhere else.

Genuine Compassion

May 22nd

Be kind; everyone you meet is struggling with something. We don't know someone until we know them. Kindness and compassion are always a wise choice.

"Genuine compassion must have both wisdom and loving compassion. One must understand the nature of the suffering from which we wish to free others (this is wisdom), and one must experience deep intimacy and empathy with other sentient beings (this is loving kindness)."
- Barbara O'Brien, *The Circle of the Way: A Concise History of Zen from the Buddha to the Modern World*

♦ Reflect on a time in your life when someone was deeply compassionate with you.

Empathy in Our DNA

May 23rd

Our nation needs to re-focus on cooperation, social responsibility, compassion, and empathy. We need to return to what unites us. We need to celebrate our strengths through diversity. We need to remember the value and worth of every single human being. Developing empathy is our challenge. What is our common good?

"Many animals survive not by eliminating each other or keeping everything for themselves, but by cooperation and sharing."
- Frans de Waal, *The Age of Empathy: Nature's Lessons for a Kinder Society*

Hopefully we are evolving from a time when only the intellectual is celebrated, and emotions are dismissed as "touchy-feely."

We are desperate to care for each other. As mammals, we survive by bonding. When we are deprived of physical and emotional caring, we die. Time with family, friends and loved ones brings us health and happiness. In times of real tragedy, such as 9/11, we forget what divides us.

We can be a fighting group of animals. A charismatic leader's ability to create discord is both historically and currently, a reality. We have potential for violence and hatred. We also have great potential for cooperation, mutual caring, and compassion. Neuroscience tells us that we are programmed to be empathetic. It is an automatic response. Only psychopaths are immune to the empathy response. The feeling of attachment is part of our limbic system, the feeling brain. The feeling brain connects us to family, friends and caring for others.

Continued...

To be empathetic, we need to understand the impact of our behavior on others. “Empathy is part of our evolution”, de Waal. We build our empathy by getting to know people and by getting closer to others’ lives and stories. We become familiar with their background and history. We all must act by supporting the dignity of every human being.

- How can you support the dignity of all the diverse students in your school?

Being Real

May 24th

In 2019, I had the privilege of speaking to 600 educators from Delaware and Maryland. This is not an uncommon experience in my life. Over the last 50 years, I have been asked to give keynote speeches and workshops. I have never thought that what I had to offer was particularly gifted or brilliant. I know that intellectually, I am very average. However, what I express resonates with most people. I share my life experiences, my heart, and my soul. I have found that being authentic and transparent does more than intellect, salesmanship, debate, or force. I find that being real, connects. My life connects with your life. My only intention is to do God's will and share my truth. As I speak, I see in the eyes and faces of the audience a genuine connection. We feel the light of our soul's sun begin to shine. We are warmed in our authenticity and vulnerability. We begin to grow together. Some call this love, some compassion, and some empathy. I feel it as community.

Somehow, through the grace of God, my vulnerability and authenticity give my listeners permission to be fully human. We remember our innocence; we remember our sense of purpose. We remember our joy.

My life is blessed to find the courage to be brave and speak my truth, to share the guidance of the still, small voice. I pray for the continued courage to be brave, to be real.

♦ With a trusted friend or loved one, share a time in your life when you were brave.

Kindness

May 25th

"Kindness and compassion are among the principal things that make our lives meaningful. Consideration of others is worthwhile because our happiness is inexplicably bound up with the happiness of others."
- His Holiness the Dalai Lama

Kindness is essential for our survival. The qualities of kindness, empathy, trust, gratitude, and forgiveness are in urgent need today and every day. The human being is hardwired for altruism. The giving of kindness benefits the receiver, the giver and all who witness kindness.

There is a great deal of hostility, negativity, and hatred in the world today. We tweet, use Facebook, Instagram, email, and watch hatred every day on TV. Mean makes headlines but humanity continues because of kindness. I see kindness every day.

In 2019, I had ear surgery at Hahnemann Hospital in Philadelphia. I felt kindness all day. My wife got up at 4:30 in the morning to drive me to surgery. Before we left our home, she got our daughter, who has special needs, ready for the day. Our youngest son, Christian, took care of his sister, including medicine, breathing treatment, and percussion vest, so we could go to the hospital for a 6:30 appointment. We entered the hospital to be shown kindness by the car attendant, the receptionist, and the surgical center registration nurse. Every question I had offered, was met with a smile. The anesthesiologist was kind and clear with his questions for me and the ear surgeon was positive and comforting. In the surgery room, the women who got me set on the operating table were all warm, friendly, clear, and kind. Until the sedation put me to sleep, all I experienced was kindness.

Continued...

In recovery, I continued to be treated with kindness and respect. I was helped, supported, and guided to the bathroom and the post op room where I got to see Sandra, my role model for kindness.

I was helped to dress, given post op instructions and a kind man wheeled me to our car. Sandra drove us home and made me soup. The rest of the day, as every day, my wife, children, and friends showered me with kindness. My loved ones are kind because it is in our DNA to be kind. So, it is for all of us. We are born to be kind.

Kindness gives meaning and value to our lives. It makes us healthy physically and psychologically. Kindness has an essential impact on our health and well-being. Kindness can transform us. It is a universal intervention. A child treated with kindness grows in health. A student treated with kindness grows to believe in themselves.

Kindness is giving up revenge and domination. Through this, we recognize other perspectives. We work to understand their point of view and challenges.

We are at a critical time in America. Kindness is essential to our survival as a people, as a nation.

♦ Reflect on a time in your life when you were shown genuine kindness.

The Time is Now!

May 26th

Everything depends on the choices we make now.
Now is *the* hour.
Now is *the* time.
We need to take responsibility.
We need to stand up.
We need to answer these essential questions.
Are you living a life that serves others?
Are you doing things that bring health and healing to the world?
Are your relationships healthy?
Are you growing?
It is time to speak your truth.
It is time to create community.
It is time to listen.
It is time to understand.

Be kind.

Do not look to the world for leadership.
Look inside yourself.

You are the leader!
Stand up!
Speak your truth!
The time is now!

- Adapted from a Hopi Elder

♦ In your home, community, or nation, where is an opportunity for you to speak your truth? Do it now.

Together We Heal

May 27th

Cutting edge physics teaches us that there is no single privileged point of view. No single perspective holds the entire truth. When we hold fast to a single point of view, we are damaging and often disrespectful. Life is a unified whole. We can only come to truth through relationship, connection, and the willingness to understand other points of view.

Einstein's theory of relativity and the core of all spiritual beliefs teaches that we are more together than alone. We need to start to live the truth of our connection. We need to recover the desire to build community. We need to heal! We must gather in community to heal our social and emotional wounds.

- In your community/school discuss connection. How is it happening? What more can be done?

Commitment

May 28th

No matter what country we originated from, no matter what our skin color, no matter what or whom we pray to, no matter what language we speak, we all want to be respected, cared for, acknowledged, and valued. Beneath all our fear and shadow, we are at our core, kind. We have more in common than different. We all need connection. We all want to belong. We all want to be understood. We all need to be loved.

I am committed to caring for every life that enters my life. I am committed to keeping my heart open. I am committed to transparency, vulnerability, authenticity, gratitude, empathy, compassion, and forgiveness.

I am committed to speaking my truth. I am committed to listening to your truth. I am committed to getting back up when I fall. I am committed to helping you up when you fall.

I am committed to…

"One nation, under God, indivisible,
with liberty and justice for All."
- Pledge of Allegiance

♦ In your school or classroom, discuss the meaning and various perspectives of justice.

Disrupting the Cycle

May 29th

"Darkness cannot drive out darkness; only light can do that. Hate cannot drive out hate; only love can do that."
- Reverend Dr. Martin Luther King Jr.

If we meet anger, hatred, and violence with a similar response than we are a part of the pain that this creates. We need to listen with a sincere intention to understand. This process of leaning into the unknown and seeking to understand will disrupt the intensity of discord.

We can disrupt the cycle of racism, anger, hatred, and violence by letting our humanity come shining through.

We need to listen, speak, and act with compassion, understanding, and love for all humanity.

♦ In what small way can you disrupt the cycle of anger, hatred, and violence?

Every Day is Your Birthday

May 30th

Today is a special day. Today, we honor a singular event in the history of the world. Your birth brought love and kindness to the world. Your life has blessed hundreds of other lives.

Today is your birthday. Choose how you wish to celebrate. Dance and sing with joy or peacefully give thanks. Do whatever is meaningful to you. Do whatever brings you joy.

You are a gift. Your unique talents, skills and visions make a difference in the world. You are a rare and beautiful gift from God. You have touched many lives, and the world is a bit better because you are here.

Thank you for your courage. Thank you for accepting the challenges of life. Every time we are vulnerable and authentic, we give others permission to be courageous and do the same. This is freedom. This brings us close to each other and close to God.

Today, count your blessings. Who has loved and supported you? What grace have you received? What beauty have you seen? What wisdom have you earned? What strength have you garnered?

Thank God for your love, your life, health, and happiness. You are blessed.

Follow the still, small voice of spirit. Follow your path. Listen to your heart's desire. Believe in yourself as God believes in you.

- ♦ Celebrate you today!

We Are Here Together

May 31st

"We live in a world where everything is connected. We can no longer think in terms of us and them when it comes to the consequences of the way we live. Today, it's all about WE."
- Gregg Braden, *Resilience from the Heart: The Power to Thrive in Life's Extremes*

We must take our essential learnings of connection, authenticity, courage, and compassion and apply them in the world. The world begins in our homes, neighborhoods, schools, workplaces, states, and country. Fear is the source of anger. Fear and anger undermine the essence of being human. There is no scenario where anger works to anyone's advantage. In fear, anger, and violence, we all lose.

The survival of our world and of our lives will not be found in fear, anger, and hatred. The loudest voice does not always win. We need to recall our existence depended upon, and still depends upon, our ability to cooperate. We need to connect. We need to listen. We need to understand.

We need to stop looking through the eyes of fear. We need to stop our obsession with us versus them. We are here together, billions of us on this round, blue, ball. In my unconditional loving God, there is a welcoming, accepting spirit. We are all one with different expressions of God's exquisite uniqueness. We can touch the world instantly. We can show love by a look, a gesture, a smile, a handshake, a hug, a phone call, an email, a tweet, or a text. We can also show love by being quiet in prayer and meditation. Breathe a message of love and change the world.

- How will you show a gesture of love today?

June

“Peace cannot be kept by force; it can only be achieved by understanding.”
~ Albert Einstein

Acceptance

June 1st

"If every person knew that they were loved and accepted by God exactly as they are right now, the world would be transformed."
- Chris Michaels, *The Power of You: 365 Daily Reflections*

We have the power to offer acceptance and emotional safety to everyone we meet. Let us embrace our differences. We are all unique emanations of God. Life is change. We are ever evolving and changing. Give yourself and others permission to change and grow.

"If we have no peace, it is because we have forgotten that we belong to each other."
- Mother Teresa

Life is consciousness unfolding. When we change our inner life, our outer life changes as well. When we do our internal, self-reflective homework, we become a vehicle for love and acceptance. Let us acknowledge and accept each other for who we are, children of God.

- Show acknowledgment and acceptance for your peers today.

Kindness and Compassion

June 2nd

"Do all the good you can, by all the means you can, in all the ways you can, in all the places you can, at all the times you can, to all the people you can, as long as you can."
- John Wesley

I find great joy in giving my life in service to others. There are many forms of generosity and service. Kind words, thoughtful actions, a compassionate smile, an emphatic touch, all these can lighten and uplift the spirit.

Our kindness and generosity are an emanation of the kindness and generosity of life. We are all connected in the spirit of kindness and compassion.

- Reflect on all the people you feel connected to.

Celebrate Life

June 3rd

I have never liked the word *tolerate*. Throughout my life, I have heard tolerance used in a variety of interpersonal, human, life challenges. It never felt right to me. It never felt human enough. I never wanted to be tolerated. I never want to be tolerant of another. Tolerance means to put up with something, to endure. I guess that is a sticking point, but I see it as on a continuum.

Tolerance- Understanding- Appreciation- Celebration.
Understanding is the beginning of peace and forgiveness.

"Seek first to understand, and then be understood."
- Stephen R. Covey, *The 7 Habits of Highly Effective People*

Understanding is the first step in unity. Appreciation of your uniqueness is the movement into the joy of life. We are different. Diversity is the spice of life. Diversity literally is life.

"…love for all living creatures is the most noble attribute of man."
- Charles Darwin

Through appreciation we know that all life is valuable. No one is more important than another. We appreciate that all of us, no matter our situation in life, have value. Celebration is the joy of togetherness, understanding and appreciation. Acceptance and appreciation of us and others leads to celebration. In celebration, we experience the beauty, honor, and glory of each individual soul.

♦ Celebrate someone else today. Tell them.

Stories

June 4th

I love stories. I love listening to, reading, and telling stories. Stories are the wealth of humanity. Stories are our heart expressing experience. Stories are how we make meaning of life. We share legacy.

When I share a story from my life, I am consumed with emotion. I am fully in the moment and in the story. I often experience the sweat and tears that bring great meaning to the story. Telling stories heals us.

There are stories about my daughter, Ashley, that I repeat often. I repeat the story to invite my listeners to be fully human. Because Ashley is so fragile and vulnerable, I comfortably share my vulnerability. Each retelling of her stories brings enhanced meaning to the experience. I continue sharing the stories that opens my heart and invites listeners to open theirs, as well. Each retelling brings me back to her angelic eyes and the Divine presence that fills her life.

I never really know what I am going to say. The story tells itself; it reveals my essence, and it saves my life again and again and again.

- Reflect on one of your favorite stories. What about this story do you love?

Loving Connection

June 5th

We must transcend the illusion of separation and realize that all humanity is one. We are all born wanting love and belonging. Connection is our birthright. When we finally discover that our value is innate to being human, we support the value of others. It is time for courageous action. We need to know that our kindness, compassion, and empathy has ripples. All our actions are contagious. We can influence our community and ultimately our world by practicing kindness, by engaging and connecting; by being compassionate and empathetic.

When we do good in the world, we do good for ourselves.

We know from the research of Dr. Barbara Fredrickson that when we create connection, our world view widens. When our perception increases, we see unity where there once was separation. Loving connection increases your circle of inclusion and concern. We become more compassionate and trusting.

Loving connection changes our hearts and minds.

- Gather with your dearest friends and trusted family and discuss-*What is essential?*
  What is our greatest task as human beings?
  What is our hope for our children?

Appreciation

June 6th

My life has taught me that all of us, all living creatures, want to be recognized. We want to be appreciated. We want to know someone is happy. We are here to share this life with them. I find it beneficial to acknowledge others by seeing them as their best self.

Spirit radiates from all life. When we recognize and appreciate each other, we all feel the healing of separation. Together, in appreciation and acknowledgement, we feel peace.

- Recognize someone today for their character and social emotional skills.

Fellowship

June 7th

"For those who have suffered, tolerance is not a political position
or even a principle; for those of us who have suffered,
who have hauled ourselves into the sun,
anything exhausted beside us is family."
- Mark Nepo, *The Book of Awakening:*
Having the Life You Want by Being Present to the Life You Have

Mark Nepo, one of my favorite authors, speaks to the comfort and fellowship of recovery and healing. Knowing we are not alone is comforting. Knowing we are not the only one is healing. In therapy, in recovery meetings, in healing circles, we listen to others tell our story. There is universality to health and healing. When we risk being authentic and vulnerable, we find that others have been down a very similar courageous path.

"We have not even to risk the adventure alone,
for the heroes of all time have gone before us.
The labyrinth is thoroughly known;
we have only to follow the thread of the hero path.
And where we had thought to find an abomination
we shall find God.
And where we had thought to slay another
we shall slay ourselves.
Where we had thought to travel outwards
we shall come to the center of our own existence.
And where we had thought to be alone
we shall be with all the world."
- Joseph Campbell, *The Hero with a Thousand Faces*

- Who is a part of your supportive, emotionally safe, trusted circle?

Together

June 8th

"It is a terrible, an inexorable, law that one cannot deny the humanity of another without diminishing one's own: in the face of one's victim one sees oneself."
- James Baldwin, *The Fire Next Time*

As a literature student I was always moved by Baldwin's writing. The above quote speaks to our challenges as a nation today. I am inspired to know that cutting edge researchers in the humanities (biology, spirituality, neuroscience, literature, and the social sciences) agree.

We are all one, we are all united.
At this point of human evolution, the only conversation of value is:
How do we work together?
How do we listen to each other?
How do we celebrate each other?
How do we love each other?

♦ In conversation with a trusted friend, dialogue and share your responses to the above four questions.

Making a Difference

June 9th

Our time and our life are precious. What are you investing your time and life in? When we are on purpose, we are connected to something larger than ourselves. We are one with life. What we do for anyone we do for everyone.

"Humankind has not woven the web of life. We are but one thread within it. Whatever we do to the web, we do to ourselves. All things are bound together. All things connect."
- Chief Seattle

"We see the universe as a solid fact. God sees it as liquid law."
- Ralph Waldo Emerson

We are all connected. Everything we do, every act we take, ripples like a stone in a pond. We are part of an interconnected universe. Like millions of educators before us, we may never know what impact we have had on others. I am always humbled when someone thanks me for something I did or said 20 or 30 years ago. When we are on purpose, we touch lives. Know that every action you take is a pebble causing ripples in a pond.

- What have you caused to ripple this past year?

We Are All Life

June 10th

We live in an interconnected universe. Every advancement we make globally impacts us personally and every improvement we make personally improves the world for everyone in our sphere of connection.

The theory of collective consciousness offers that anything we give to the world returns to us. We all add to life when we make efforts to benefit life. When we serve others, we all benefit. The giver, the receiver, and the observers of kindness and service all benefit. We are all connected. We are all life.

- ♦ Reflect on the interconnectedness of your life. What surprises you?

Endless Immigration

June 11th

We all lead lives of endless immigration. I find as I grow and develop, I am always arriving in new lands.

Working towards becoming a good man leads me constantly to new experiences. When I became a husband, I immigrated to the country of Sandra, her family and all the blessings of her unconditional love. When I had children, I entered the world of fatherhood. I am still trying to find my comfort in this country. I sometimes feel judged for being other than what others want me to be. In the world of work, I am a nomad moving from mission to mission; each service point, an oasis of purpose and meaning. Many friends have welcomed me into the hearts of their country. Some have asked me to leave.

I am aware we are all immigrants. We will always be leaving one shore to find another. This life has been a great adventure. There is still one more leaving and entering.

- Where in your life have you felt like an immigrant?
- What have these lessons taught you?

Legacy

June 12th

A star shining in the night's sky gives all its energy constantly, providing light in the darkness. Science tells us that not only does it produce light during its lifetime, but also, it's light shines long after the star is gone. The star did not need to be known. It did not need to be celebrated. It didn't even need to be named. It fulfilled its purpose by simply shining.

We are here for the same purpose; to shine our light. Being fully present. This is our purpose. When we give our presence to all that we touch, our life grows. We glow through our service to humanity.

Our bodies will pass away.

Our legacy will live forever.

- Whose legacy are you a part of?
- Whose shining light are you now passing on to others?

Kindness

June 13th

Simple kindness to all life and to oneself is the most powerful transformational force I have been privileged to witness. My wife, Sandra, is my daily example of unconditional kindness.

Her kindness has no downside as it supports everyone and everything. Her kindness, lessons of grief, loss, and stress all have depth and meaning. Sandra's kindness is endless joy, happiness, and contentment. It increases true power without the toll of force. There are no exceptions to Sandra's kindness. Her kindness is pure, service oriented. She has no thought for her own reward. It is because of her altruism that she is spiritually rewarded.

- Show appreciation for your role models of loving kindness.

Unity

June 14th

"In one atom are found all the elements of the earth; in one motion of the mind are found all the motions of existence; in one drop of water are found all the secrets of the endless oceans; in one aspect of you are found all the aspects of life."
- Kahlil Gibran

This is beautiful writing. We are each in a single atom. We are each part of the earth. In my mind, I am giving birth, and I am dying. I am creating and growing, and I am letting go and saying goodbye. I am a part of you, and you are a part of me. Unity.

I open and close my heart and mind countless times a day.

This is the ongoing dance of balance between ego and spirit.

- In discussion with a colleague or peer group, discuss your thoughts on unity.

Share Your Heart

June 15th

The sun sparks,
love reaches out it's hand and places it,
gently upon your face.
Your fear becomes insignificant.
Heart to heart,
each to the other.
This is the greatest beauty in the world.
Joy.
Unity.
Blessing.

- Inspired by Hafiz

- ♦ Reach out your hand to a loved one and share your heart.

Awakening to the Truth: We Are All One in Love

June 16th

I have lived long enough to see-
hate fade from the eyes of men and women as they are forgiven.

I have lived long enough to see-
men and women of difference holding hands in similarity.

I have lived long enough to hear-
the one song that we all sing as we recognize our unity in the Divine.

I have lived long enough to experience-
men and women so committed to love they would choose to die before being unkind.

I have lived long enough to see-
hatred fade from the eyes of men and women when they are aware that they cannot hurt another without also hurting themselves.

- Speak your truth in a group meeting and listen to the truth of others.

Hate Will Dissipate and Be Broken by Love

June 17th

If we stand up to hate, the world will be blessed with a freedom never known before.

If we fail to speak our truth,
if we fail to stand up to hate with love,
the whole world,
including everyone we know and love and all those we care for,
will sink into a depth known in history as the holocaust.

Let us pray together in love and respect and care,
and believe and accept one another,
no matter how different.

- Do not let the historical truths of human love and hate be dismissed. Speak the truth of history.

Storytelling

June 18th

Stories are the wealth of humanity. There have been times in my life when my pockets and wallet were empty. There has never been a time when my heart and soul were empty.

My life has been full of story, and I feel a legacy, a calling, to pass them on. They carry the essential truth and meaning of life, my life and I, believe your life. Our stories are connected. Each telling of our story renews our lives; and each retelling of the story brings us healing.

I have told and retold the story of our daughter Ashley's life repeatedly. Her lessons are deep, profound, and meaningful. I find telling her story gives permission to others to tell their story. When people listen to Ashley's story, they allow themselves to be vulnerable; and in this vulnerability, healing begins. Every telling of Ashley's story re-opens my heart; and it opens the hearts of all who listen.

Before I speak to an audience, large or small, I close my eyes, go inside, and pray: "Please God, your will, not mine, be done."

I am free, I am open, I am healed, and with the grace of God, the story I tell brings healing to you.

♦ What story in your life, when told, will resonate with other stories?

Empathy and Compassion

June 19th

Empathy is feeling with another person. Compassion takes the next step in human evolution and acts on that feeling of unity consciousness.

Compassion is our way of being in the world. Compassion moves to create truth and love. Compassion moves us to responsibility and asks us to experience different truths.

Our compassion originates in unconditional love for self and others. We know we are all connected. Compassion seeks the highest good for all.

- In quiet reflection, think of someone you feel disconnected from.
- How do they need your compassion?
- Send love to them with a few deep, long breaths.

Story

June 20th

Stories are our wealth. They are the wealth of our heart and soul. They are filled with our truth, our experience, our beliefs, our values, and our history. When we tell our story, our authenticity grows and deepens. There is a great healing when we share our story. Both the tellers and listeners are healed as we realize we are not alone. As we tell our story, we give others permission to tell theirs.

Most of what I do as a public speaker is tell my story. I tell my family's story. I share my vulnerability, authenticity, and my truth. Although I have a plan when I begin, each speech is a different story. The story reveals my heart. Each telling of my story saves me. With each breath, the story is the same and different. I find that as I share my story, it gives others the invitation to do the same.

- With a trusted friend, share your story and listen to their story.

Being Human

June 21st

No other form of life has the depth of intellect and consciousness that human beings are privileged to experience. The Buddhists believe it is a rare gift to be born a human. We as humans have the ability to write and read these words. To feel connected emotionally through these words is rare indeed. I never want to take the gift of this human life for granted.

Today we are alive. Today we share our precious and rare humanity. I am grateful to be here with you. Today we have much to be thankful for. Today we are awake. We are grateful to feel the warmth of the sun and the warmth of those we love.

- How will you act today?
- How will you feel today?
- Who will you connect with today?

Our Life is a Gift

June 22nd

Our life is a gift. I am grateful every day that I get to live this beautiful life. I have learned that to retain my gift of life, I need to give it away. I need to give my life in service to the world. We can all make a gift of our lives when we are kind with those who cross our path. I give the gift of life when I am understanding, compassionate, empathetic, forgiving, and generous. We all benefit when we share these life affirming gifts. Giving of ourselves and our humanity is the best gift we can give.

- How are you giving the gift of life to those you most care about?

The Family of Love

June 23rd

We are all here for a short time; twenty, forty, sixty, eighty, one hundred years. We are here to love and be loved. We are here to learn and relearn that we are all children of unconditional love.

We are here to help us all remember who we are. We are here to remember we are all members of one beloved family.

We are here to break down walls and build bridges. Walls are built on fear. Bridges are built on unity. In our unity, we are all here for just a little while to remember to love and be loved.

We are all members of the family of love.

- With a trusted friend, discuss a time in your life when you built a bridge or broke down a wall to make connection.

What is Your School Community's Shared Story?

June 24th

When we make a commitment to build community, we create "we" stories. We honor and value each other's courage and vulnerability and we share our skills and strengths in service to the greater good.

We share leadership. We reclaim our power to help ourselves. We do not wait for permission. When we see a human need, we fill it. We prioritize the community's good over individual ego. We emphasize connection. We share food, laughter, tears, and dreams. We plan for the future and implement now!

We practice gratitude and forgiveness. We know we are servant leaders. We know our community is defined by how we care for the young, old, poor, disabled, and those who are sad and disconnected. We take responsibility and apologize when we make mistakes.

"The secret of life is to have a task, something you devote your entire life to, something you bring everything to, every minute of every day, for the rest of your life. And the most important thing, is it must be something you cannot possibly do."
- Henry Moore

- Share with a group of trusted colleagues how you could save your school community. How can you fill a need?

We Are All Different

June 25th

Life is a gift.

We are each blessed with our spirit and our divine uniqueness. We are each different. If we look close enough, we see everything, and everyone is different. We can find similarities but none of us are the same.

We all bring our unique light to the world. We all shine differently. The moon does not complain that it is not as bright as the sun. The moon does not feel less than the sun. We must stop comparing, judging, and evaluating each other.

Trust that your uniqueness is needed in the world. We are all different. Each of us expressing our uniqueness to make the world a better place. Happiness is sharing your gift and your unique way.

- Reflect and journal about how you are unique and how this uniqueness can save the world.

Compassion

June 26th

Compassion is at the heart of all the good that human beings have done in the world.

Compassion calls us to serve, uplift, and support others as we would wish to be served, uplifted, and supported.

Compassion demands that we work to end the pain of our fellow humans and to honor the sacredness of every human life.

We are called to treat every human being with justice, fairness, respect, equity, and compassion.

- What act of compassion do you feel called to enact? Commit to this compassionate action now.

Friendship

June 27th

The best way to have a friend is to be a friend.

Being in a friendship is one of the most essential human relationships. The connection, bonding, and intimacy is a sharing of self at a level that invites us into deep learning. Healthy friendships help us become the best possible versions of ourselves.

My dearest friends encouraged my authenticity, vulnerability, and courage. They also forgive me when I make mistakes and fall flat on my face. I also forgive them when they stumble in the human journey.

I continue to learn how to create healthy boundaries through my friendships. We teach people how to treat us by making it clear what we will accept and not accept. Through the development of truth and trust, we make clear our agreements on how we will love and support each other.

◆ Write a letter to one of your closest friends and share specifically the character traits that you admire in them.

Sharing our Stories

June 28th

The exploration of our shared humanity is a privilege that I have been deeply committed to for my past 71 years.

Each day, I begin my exploration with meditation, self-reflection, and assessment. I deliberately focus on the good I can give and the good I will receive. I have a genuine interest in the people I meet and interact with throughout my day. I do my best to smile and have a positive attitude. I strive to be a good listener and focus on remembering people's names. I think calling someone by name is a sign of respect.

I love to listen to other's stories. We all have a life story. I believe our stories are our wealth. I feel that our stories reveal that we are more similar than different. In the sharing of our stories, I find perspective, understanding, compassion, and empathy.

I encourage all of us to embrace our story; speak our truth. In speaking our truth and sharing our story, we are all able to listen to other truths and embrace other stories. We will feel the unity and diversity. We are hardwired for connection.

"Authentic social connection has a profound effect on your mental health - it even exceeds the value of exercise and an ideal body weight on your physical health."
- Dr. James Doty, *Into the Magic Shop: A Neurosurgeon's Quest to Discover the Mysteries of the Brain and the Secrets of the Heart*

Kindness, respect, understanding, compassion, and empathy is good for everyone.

- Share your love with humanity.

Love is Transformational

June 29th

"God does not love us if we change.
God loves us so we can change."
- Richard Rohr

Love is the most powerful, transformational tool we have in our life toolkit.

Love may come in the form of a deeply listening friend. It may come to you as firm boundaries offered by a trusted confidant. Love may come in the form of creative expression or a blast of energy to complete a project. Love can come as a firm no or a sweet yes.

Every expression of love is transformational.

- Pay attention to how love, in all its forms, is coming to you today.

Listen

June 30th

"When you listen deeply, you help people suffer less."
- Thich Nhãt Hanh

We all appreciate and need a true listener. Someone who will offer a non-judgmental listening ear. When we open our hearts, we do not ask to be fixed. We ask for kindness, understanding, and compassion.

"Compassion is not a relationship between the healer and the wounded. It's a relationship between equals. Only when we know our darkness well can we be present with the darkness of others. Compassion becomes real when we recognize our shared humanity."
- Pema Chödrön, *The Places That Scare You: A Guide to Fearlessness in Difficult Times*

Compassion allows us to feel our connectedness, it allows us to feel our unity. We are one.

Let us listen with a soft heart and an open mind.

Let us be a safe place for anyone to share their vulnerability.

- Who needs you to listen to them?

Relationship Skills

July and August

"Our skills to build relationships help us build connection. Human beings are hard-wired for connection."
- Dr. Brené Brown, *Daring Greatly: How the Courage to Be Vulnerable Transforms the Way We Live, Love, Parent, and Lead*

Relationship Skills help us to build trust, to learn to cooperate, and collaborate to solve problems. Relationship Skills help us resolve conflicts and develop positive relationships. Relationship Skills help us create caring leaders and well informed, empathetic followers. We are able to say no to social pressure, offer help when it is needed, and celebrate diverse cultures.

July

"Perfect kindness acts without thinking of kindness."
~ Lao Tso

Connection

July 1st

One of the greatest human needs, along with food, water, and shelter is touch. We are biologically designed to nurture, connect, and feel the loving touch of another.

It is through the human power of kindness and connection that we will solve the challenges of the world. I am no longer enamored with intellect. I know too many very bright intellectuals doing little to help the world and the people in the world. I also know countless individuals whose compassion, empathy, and kindness has touched hearts, minds, and saved lives. We have the power to be warm, caring, sensitive, understanding, and open. These profound human character traits bring a deep heartfelt caring for the value of every precious human life.

We all need compassion. In our pain and grief, we are healed by the loving presence of another human being. Love is the greatest of all human strengths. Love transforms our pain into forgiveness, gratitude, and integrity. We are all blessed with our own personal stories of challenge, compassion, and growth. I invite each of us to reflect on a time in your lives when you were compassionate. Allow yourself to remember the feel and warmth of extending compassion and love to another human being. These are the transformational moments of life- those single moments of trusting, listening, saying "I love you", holding a hand, and giving a hug. These are the finest moments of human connection.

- ♦ Please share an experience when you were the recipient of kindness or compassion.

Connection and Community: Essential to Our Well-Being

July 2nd

In the past five years, I am finding more adult students in our master's courses and professional development programs who are genuinely excited to be invited into an authentic community building experience.

Psychology and physiology tell us we need each other to be healthy and to thrive. We need true community for health and happiness. We gather to celebrate our shared humanity and we gather to heal our shared wounds.

Community and connection promote health, while Dr. James House of University of Michigan says, "…isolation fosters stress, disease, and death. Social isolation is as dangerous as smoking, high blood pressure, high cholesterol, obesity, and lack of exercise."

Connection and community are essential to our well-being.

- ♦ How are you building connection and community in staff and students? Please share two specifics that you can pass on to your administrative colleagues.

Relationships and Teachings

July 3rd

"The beginning of love is to let those we love to be perfectly themselves, and not twist them to fit our own image. Otherwise, we love only the reflection of ourselves we find in them."
- Thomas Merton, *No Man Is an Island*

Relationships teach us everything about life. We soar, we fall, we love, we anger, we find truth and betrayal, we are compassionate, and we can be cruel. I believe we must continually open the door to our hearts and minds to learn and to heal. Every lesson teaches, every lesson transforms.

Spirit teaches us-
we are all one,
we are all beloved.

- How are you purposefully building relationships in your school?

A Shared Beat

July 4th

"If you place two living heart cells from two different people
in a petri dish, they will, in time,
find and maintain a third and common beat."
- Molly Vass

Hidden in our biology is the secret power of relationships. The essence of life is to join.

This is love.
This is life.

Share your compassion. It is only natural; it is what we were designed to do. It does not matter how different we are. Inside we all search for connection; we yearn to beat in unison with others.

Share your heart's song and invite others to sing along.

- What song speaks to your heart?

Empathy and Trust: The Standards for Which We Must Strive

July 5th

We must see everyone in our schools as a human being. Everyone! This includes students (ALL students), teachers (regular education, special education, health, and physical education), custodial staff, administrative assistants, food service workers, paraprofessionals, administrators, and especially parents. We must remember that education is personal to every one of our students. We are all human beings with fears and talents.

Empathy and trust must be the standards for which we strive. Empathy is the essential connection we experience when we feel *with someone*. It is the single greatest asset in education and in life; empathy brings a long-lasting feeling of all the good that exists and reassures human beings that they are not alone. To earn trust, we must extend trust. We must believe in the goodness of people, and we need to treat them as if they are that goodness. We must lead with our hearts as well as with our minds. We must see test scores, academic standards, and budgets as subordinate to people and not the other way around. In my experience, all three of these have, at different times, been seen as more important than the people in the organization. If we're ever going to reach our goals for children and learning, human connection and empathy must be our highest priority.

The only way to advance education is for people to pull together as a community and focus on empathy, to build trust, and respect for everyone. We need to rebuild schools that have, as their highest priority, the care of human beings.

◆ What behaviors do people show you that generate trust? What behaviors are you exhibiting that invite others to trust you?

The World is Waiting

July 6th

The world is waiting to hear your inner voice, waiting for your greatness. Only God knows what you're capable of. Do what brings you the greatest joy and the world will be grateful for your sharing. If the world does not understand, let it go. God will understand. It is only about you and God anyway.

◆ Reflect on what brings you joy. What would you do for nothing? Follow your bliss.

Steps to Respond with Compassion

July 7th

"From your brain's perspective, treating people around you with kindness is usually, but not always, the right response."
- Dr. Paul Zak, *The Trust Factor: The Science of Creating High-Performance Companies*

Compassion improves behavior. Throughout my 50 years in education, I have often investigated and discussed with fellow educators what is our best intervention for a student who is underperforming or behaving inappropriately. In my 20's, I sometimes responded with anger and frustration. Expressing my frustration was a very honest reaction and allowed an outlet for my stress. It may have stopped the behavior for a short period of time because they were frightened; but overall, not helpful. Generally, I have found that punishment is not the answer to challenging behavior. I have grown to the place that in my 70's, I focus on compassion and curiosity.

Compassion and curiosity ask, "What happened to you?" Compassion and curiosity move me from the judgmental place of "What's wrong with you?"

Current research in Trauma Informed Practices and empathy tells me compassion will be the better intervention. Compassion and curiosity will initiate connection, build relationships, and build trust and loyalty. Students will see their teachers as kind and this kindness *"elevates"* their trust and loyalty.

"Trust profoundly improves performance by providing the foundation for effective teamwork and intrinsic motivation."
- Dr. Paul Zak, *The Trust Factor: The Science of Creating High-Performance Companies*

Continued...

Research also tells us that not only will the student who receives our compassion and curiosity be elevated, but all the students who witness our compassion will also increase their trust and loyalty and be elevated as well.

Compassion increases human beings' desire and willingness to trust. Neuroscience confirms; trust improves behavior and performance. Compassion also reduces the students' stress response. The reduction in stress and the increase in trust increases creativity, learning, and innovation.

Steps to Respond with Compassion
-*Take a* Breath. We need to take a pause and breathe. We need to control our initial fight, flight, or freeze response. Pausing to take a breath invites a more mindful response.

-*Empathize*. We need to see the whole child and be aware of all that is impacting their life and current behavior.

-*Forgive*. Forgiveness strengthens our connection and relationship. Forgiveness builds trust. Forgiveness lowers your blood pressure and that of the person you are forgiving. Forgiveness reduces stress.

-*Compassion.* Compassion produces connection, trust, loyalty, creativity, learning, and innovation. Compassion lowers stress and improves our overall health and well- being.

"We don't have to earn the right to compassion;
it is our birthright."
- Dr. Kristin Neff, *Self-Compassion:*
The Proven Power of Being Kind to Yourself

♦ Reflect on how compassion can reduce your stress level. Share your thoughts in a journal or with a friend.

Every Life is a Blessing

July 8th

Ashley lived longer and more vibrantly than anyone expected. Her life is a miracle.

She has come in her wheelchair, to a few of my speeches over the course of her 39 years. I have spoken across the continent, and I have shared her story everywhere. Her presence, her story, and her life have touched the hearts of tens of thousands.

Ashley emanates Divine love. She is pure in her body, mind, and spirit. She has no ego. Her challenges are obvious. No physical movement, no vocal ability, no ability to eat, drink, or swallow. Her one ability is love, unconditional love.

We, her immediate family, have grown familiar with her routines. Sleep, wake, medication, feedings, breathing treatments, percussion, transfer to wheelchair, repeat, repeat, repeat for 39 years. Ashley is open and loving to all treatment. She is open and loving to all life. Her deep brown eyes shine with the light of her soul. Being in her presence is a great blessing. In Ashley's presence, I feel the unconditional love of Divinity.

I have learned to never take a moment of life for granted. It is a privilege to be in her presence. I have learned to never hold anything back. I tell her with each interaction, I love her, and I am grateful to be with her.

Every life is a blessing.
Let those we love know that we love them.
Take nothing and no one for granted.

◆ With one of your most trusted relationships, let them know how much you love and value them.

One Unconditional Loving Soul

July 9th

"Intimate attachments to other human beings are the hub around which a person's life revolves…from these intimate attachments a person draws his strength and enjoyment of life and, through what he contributes, he gives strength and enjoyment to others."
- John Bowlby, *Attachment and Loss, Volume 1: Attachment*

"Neuroscientists now understand that this attunement- this mysterious alignment of minds- is in fact, the central ingredient in secure attachment… it is the very essence of connection."
- Stephen Cope, *The Great Work of Your Life: A Guide for the Journey to Your True Calling*

This intimate attachment, attunement, alignment, and connection is exactly what I feel with and for my wife Sandra. Sandra has the ability to perceive the needs of others. She understands their concerns and challenges and responds with compassion and love. She lets us know that we are needed in this world and assures us that we are accepted, just the way we are.

We all need this kind of secure attachment. We all need one unconditional loving soul to share the moments of our life. We only need one- that one could be in a moment, or they could be in a lifetime. Whatever the experience, this secure attachment acts as a repair kit.

"There is a possibility of connection and repair everywhere…the self is profoundly self-repairing. Like a seed, the self seeks the ground in which it can grow.
- Stephen Cope, *The Great Work of Your Life: A Guide for the Journey to Your True Calling*

- To whom are you most *securely* attached? Let them know.

The Power of Touch

July 10th

The following is from *The Rabbit Effect: Live Longer, Happier, and Healthier with the Groundbreaking Science of Kindness,* by Dr. Kelli Harding.

"Oxytocin is known as the 'love hormone' because it's involved in bonding, empathy, and trust. It is released at childbirth and during breastfeeding; as well as when we hug, kiss, and snuggle.

Oxytocin helps us remember faces and build connection; and it increases steadily during the first six months of parenting for moms and dads. Oxytocin helps us to feel calm, appreciated, and even to sing more. There's a biological reason that a friends' supportive hand on your shoulder, or a pat on the back comforts us.

The sense of connection from touch is more than emotional attachment. There's a psychological factor. Holding hands lowers our blood pressure, heart rate, and cortisol."

This powerful research encourages me to continue to speak to the power and importance of connection. How do we connect? We connect with a high five, fist bump, handshake, hug, or a pat on the back. Maybe connection is through the eyes- a long, sustained, listening with sincere eye contact. We must continue to create connection and build relationships with our students and our colleagues. Relationships are the most important part of a happy, healthy, and successful life. We must invest time and energy in building classroom and school relationships.

We all need to be loved.

♦ How are you letting your students know you care about them and their lives?

The Box

July 11th

Sometimes our families, co-workers, schools, religions, and society put us in a box, one that makes them comfortable. Sometimes the box will fit us just fine. Sometimes, it will not work.

If your work, relationships, dreams, and ambitions are not approved by others, you do not have a problem. You are not the problem. If the box does not fit your dreams, adapt the box, or move out.

"It is not the most intellectual of the species that survives;
but the species that survives is the one
that is best able to adapt and adjust."
- Leon C. Megginson, *Interpreting Darwin*

Do not suffocate yourself trying to fit into something that does not suit you. You know what feels right. If you are full of joy, creativity, zest for life, passion, and purpose then you have found the right fit.

All those who truly love you will want you to be happy.

♦ Reflect on your passion and purpose. Are you living your passion and purpose.

Choose Love, Choose Life, Choose Renewal

July 12th

When we stay with something (relationship, occupation, etc.) too long that does not nurture us, we begin to suffer. Our work suffers, our relationships suffer, and most importantly, our spirit suffers. The challenge is deciding when we keep trying or when it's time to let go and say good-bye.

Sometimes we are asked to dig deeper into a relationship; to love more, to trust more, to renew and to refresh.

Sometimes we are being asked to let go; to say goodbye, to move on to something new. Do not continue to invest in what is not healthy.

Choose love,
Choose life,
Choose renewal.

- What choices are you making today that are life affirming?

My Truth

July 13th

The whole world could praise my friend and he wouldn't feel better than anyone else. The whole world could criticize my friend and it wouldn't affect him in the least. He was clear that all his work was internal. He had no control over anyone's opinion of him. He had total responsibility of his internal awareness and growth.

I still let the opinions of others affect me. I am pleased that I still care deeply about how people feel. I am still trying to care less about what they think of me.

I have committed my life to God's will. I follow God's still, small voice. This truth moves from my inside to the world outside. I want to be liked, I want to avoid conflict, I want to be understood. Most importantly, I want to be comfortable in my own skin. I follow my soul's song. I only know my truth.

♦ In conversation with a trusted friend, discuss how the opinions of others affect you.

Our Universal Communication

July 14th

Research tells us that the human organism needs 6-8 respectful loving touches a day to survive. We know that premature infants gain more weight in the first two weeks of life when prescribed "tactile, kinesthetic stimulation" (loving touch). Touch to a premature infant means weight gain; weight gain means life. Touch heals. The pains of life dissipate when we are hugged and comforted.

Touch is our universal communication. It crosses all linguistic and religious boundaries. All prejudice, fear, and hatred crumble in the presence of compassion. Touch is as essential as breath. Without breath, we suffocate; without touch, we wither and die.

Deep within each of us there is a need to be touched, comforted, supported, and loved. We need this for each other. We must give and receive loving touch.

- How do you express your caring and compassion for others?
- How do you prefer to receive expressions of care and compassion from others?

Love is Who We Are

July 15th

Love is who we are. It is not simply an emotion. It is not only something we give. It does not have to be deserved; love is God's grace in action. We are love and the more we share love, the more it increases in us, in others, in the world; it increases. Love is transformational. Love is the heart of gratitude and forgiveness. We express love when we acknowledge and appreciate others in our life.

Love is our natural, God given state. It is the way we were designed to be in the world. As we see others in love, we are seen as well. The more we give love, the more love we have to give.

- Today, who in your life needs your expression of love?

The Healthy Community

July 16th

The healthy community is measured by its passion for *all* its members.

The healthy community seeks to understand all its members. Community asks us to invest our time and energy in one another. Community nurtures, supports, cares for, and holds each other responsible.

I am my sibling. I am my parent. I am my caregiver. I am every member of my community.

Listen to understand.
Listen to forgive.
Listen to love.

- Who needs to be included in your community?
- Reach out and include someone who needs you now.

Honor All People

July 17th

When I was a little boy, there was a newspaper comic strip called "Pogo", created by Walt Kelly. The classic line in the comic was:

"We have met the enemy and they is us."

We must focus on discernment. We must focus on devotion and selfless service. Children of God we are here for more than self-gratification. Service offers peace. Self-gratification leads to pain. If we want peace, we must follow our inner, spiritual voice. This voice recalls our heritage as sons and daughters of God.

We must be true and faithful to that within us that knows the truth.

We cannot give and receive the gifts that God has lovingly given if we are self-absorbed. God made us all. Every one of us is a child of God. We are designed to connect. Dr. Brené Brown, in her research, has shown human beings are hard-wired for connection. We break the human connection when we are self-centered. We can restore our connection through service, by giving our time, attention, and talents in service to someone in need.

"Honor all people."
- 1 Peter 2:17, *The Holy Bible, New King James Version*

♦ What actions can you take today to honor everyone you interact with?

Thank You for Being with Us

July 18th

Every day when I go for a walk, I breathe in the fresh air and appreciate the sunlight on my shoulders. I consciously smile and or say hello to everyone I see passing.

It has become very important to me, especially now, to say something kind; to let people know that there is emotional safety in the world.

I experience my heart physically and emotionally. I want to be as authentic and real as possible as I walk along the path.

When I see old friends I embrace them, when I return home, I hug my beloved wife; reminding her of all the joy and love she brings into my life.

I want love and affection to pour from my eyes the way the sun warms my shoulders.

I want to continue to learn from children. I want to continue to care deeply for my friends. I want to sing, write poetry, and remind everyone we are children of God. We are all evolving. We are all becoming.

When I awake each morning, I stop in our daughter's room. I adjust the feeding tube and her monitors, bend down, and kiss her head and whisper in her ear, "I love you! I love you!" I make the sign of the cross on her forehead and thank her for being with us.

I want to thank everyone for being with us. I love you.

- Who in your life needs your expression of gratitude?

LOVE

July 19th

"The one thing we can never get enough of is love.
And the one thing we can never give enough of is love."
- Henry Miller

"I am reminded that everything we do is either an act of love or cry for love. Love works. Love is connection, and we as humans are hardwired for connection."
- Dr. Brené Brown

Love comes in many forms; the joy of seeing a baby smile, the expression of the reception of gratitude, the serenity of being in the company of someone with whom you can be fully authentic, the genuine interest we express to someone we share a passion with, the inspiration when seeing another human meet and conquer a life threatening challenge, the awe of an Arizona desert sunset, the transformation of a life spent together with a human being who accepts you unconditionally.

All of us want and need to know we are loved. To love ourselves and to love each other connects us to the unconditional love of Divinity.

"Love is the only sane and satisfactory response
to the challenges of life."
- Erich Fromm, *The Art of Loving*

♦ Make a list of all the people, places, and experiences you love. Revisit this list often and be aware of how you feel.

Give and Receive Love

July 20th

The essential thing to teach and learn is love. We must uncover our original core as human beings. We are here in this human life to give and receive love.

It is through being fully human that we learn to love. It is only through relationships that we learn what is essential. We must open our hearts to vulnerability, authenticity, and courage. Every relationship will transform us. Life tells us that we are renewed in relationships. Our essence is found in relationships. The meaning of life is found in meaningful relationships. Love is found in relationships- love of self, love of the sacred others, love of the earth, love of life, love of God.

- How in your life have you accepted others just the way they are?
- How have you at other times tried to change others?
- Reflect on the feelings you have received from both behaviors.

Kindness

July 21st

If you see someone being courageous, let them know. They might be moving through a tremendous amount of doubt and challenge.

If you see someone being compassionate, let them know. They may be coming through a time of sadness or loss.

When we reach out and share our love, we help others see how lovable they truly are. Kindness is the strongest cure. Kindness is one of the most powerful forces in the universe. Bright and warm as the sun, it melts the ice and snow of betrayal, anger, hurt, and distrust. Kindness is the antidote to broken relationships.

When we have been hurt and wounded, as we repair, we are best served by being kind. When given an opportunity to recommit, speak with kindness. When attempting to let go and move ahead, act with kindness.

With kindness, we start to soften. With kindness, we see perspective. With kindness, we can stand in our truth. With kindness, we can claim our integrity. With kindness, we become one.

♦ Today, let someone know you see their courage, let them know you see their compassion.

Kindness is not a Luxury. It is a Necessity.

July 22nd

Practicing kindness is good for our psychology and good for our physiology. Practicing kindness is good for the recipient and good for the giver.

Dr. David Hamilton shows in his research that human beings are hardwired to be kind, and our physical bodies are at their peak of health when we practice kindness. It has been repeatedly proven that our bodies respond to and need kindness.

"Being kind actually changes the
internal biochemistry of your body."
- Dr. David Hamilton, *The Five Side Effects of Kindness: This Book Will Make You Feel Better, Be Happier & Live Longer*

Kindness increases our positivity and leads to better physical health and inward happiness. Our survival as human beings have historically and continually been dependent upon the kindness of others. Human beings survive because we are kind and because we show kindness. Kindness is a matter of common sense. By practicing kindness, we ensure our benefit and the benefit of our loved ones and community. Our health and happiness are inherently connected to the health and happiness of others.

Cruelty and violence make the news headlines because they are the exception. The world evolves because we take care of each other. Compassion after natural tragedies proves life goes on, and precisely because we are kind to each other. Kindness is not a luxury; it is a necessity.

- Spend a day practicing kindness and monitor your physical, social, and emotional well-being.

Kindness Evolution

July 23rd

We are united.
I am in you; you are in me.

When our egos are worn down, it is hard to tolerate narcissism.
When humbled, it is a challenge to be around self-centeredness.

Our service to others burns away all elitism.
Kindness is the next evolutionary norm.

Giving and receiving love transforms us.
We are lovable, we are loving, and we all make mistakes.

Mistakes are simply another opportunity to be kind to yourself and others.

- What was your most recent mistake?
- What did you learn from this experience?

Everybody Matters

July 24th

"Every single employee is someone's son or daughter. Like a parent, a leader of a company is responsible for their precious lives."
- Bob Chapman

As educators, our students are our children. We are all responsible for "their precious lives". Educational leaders are likewise responsible for the "precious lives" of everyone on their staff.

Every day, we must make the time to show our students, our colleagues, our support staff, and our parents that we care and that they are important in our lives. We need to acknowledge their value and the positive impact they have on our schools and on the lives of our children. We need to acknowledge educators for their patience, perseverance, and passion. We need to acknowledge our support staff for their caring, consistency, and compassion. We need to acknowledge our administration for their leadership, humility, and faith in us. We need to acknowledge parents for their belief in us, their trust in us, and their love for their children. We need to acknowledge children for their effort, for their creativity, and for their honesty.

We need to affirm and to value every human life. We need to inspire and to help them achieve their dreams. Our caring affirmations and empathy can become contagious. This positive contagion will leave our classrooms, schools, families, community, and world a little bit better.

- How do you let students and staff members know you care about them?

"It's Just Business"

July 25th

This is the biggest falsehood in human interaction.

Business is human interaction.
Business is winning and losing.
Business is growing and declining.
Business is acquisitions, mergers, transitions, closures.

Trust is an essential ingredient in human business and human interaction.
To earn trust, we must extend trust.
We must believe in the goodness of people.
We must lead with our hearts as well as our heads.

A successful business is not just business; it is a family. We need to treat people like family, not as employees. We are in a relationship and relationships are the essence of human growth and development.

We need to rebuild schools, not as a business, but as a family.
We need to rebuild schools, that have as their highest priority, the care of human beings.

♦ In conversation with colleagues, brainstorm the traits of a healthy family. Compare your list to your school culture. In what ways is a healthy family like a healthy school?

Sandra and Ashley

July 26th

I have watched in awe as Sandra has cared for Ashley, our special needs daughter, for the past 39 years.

Sandra is a saint to our daughter. Ashley is an angel. I do not write these words figuratively. I mean them literally. I have been a witness to this unconditional, divine love for 39 years. Sandra and I were told early in Ashley's development:

"She will never be normal."
"She will never be successful."
"She will never be useful or productive."
"She will never meet any societal standards."

Through Sandra's love and Ashley's divine presence, we have risen above the limiting beliefs and cruel diagnosis that would make someone feel less valuable and invisible. We have been blessed to participate in a divine reality of unconditional love.

Ashley is a very precious soul. She has profound value in her quiet, peaceful existence. She is cherished by Sandra and I and our extended family and friends. She is cherished as a precious child of God.

In Ashley's presence, you feel close to God. There is a palpable unconditional loving presence. When you are in the presence of a soul who does not know judgement, you can be fully authentic. There is a blessed freedom that we feel when we can be our true self. You feel that freedom, blessing and grace in Ashley and Sandra's presence.

- Who are the human saints and angels in your life?

Every Day, Every Moment, An Opportunity to Love

July 27th

My life is devoted to helping each of us and myself understand we are all worthy of love just because we are. Our birthright is love, to love and be loved. Every interaction is an opportunity to love- a respectful handshake, a pat on the back, a hug and deeply paying attention and listening to someone. We need to be aware; we need to be conscious. There are no small actions. Everything we do, everything we say, everything we think and feel, matters to someone.

Every day, every moment is an opportunity to love.

- Who and how will you love today?

A Thought

July 28th

The only sane, satisfying, and sustainable option for humanity is to live with compassion, empathy, and kindness.

♦ Today, be conscious to act with compassion, empathy, and kindness.

Ashley

July 29th

My dear quiet angel. Are you aware that you have changed the world simply by sitting quietly in your wheelchair? Your constant unconditional loving meditation and prayer has blessed my life and every life that has been in your presence. Your unconditional love is always pulsating, giving, and receiving. You have achieved your destiny. There's so much Divinity in your kind and gentle spirit.

You are always near. The touch of your hand is softer than the finest silk. Your infrequent sounds dance across my ears and smiles break out of my face. I am blessed to be in your presence. The greatest gift I have ever received in my life, along with your mom, is your life.

- Sit quietly and reflect on the unique, different souls in your life.
- How have you become a better person because of these souls?

Togetherness

July 30th

"You know the first moment of dawn has arrived when you look into the eyes of another human being and see yourself."
- *The Talmud*

This spiritual experience is what human beings were created for. We are hardwired for connection. Empathy is our birthright. We are more alike than we are different.

In the master's courses I teach, I love to explore everything that everyone in the class has in common. I also love to celebrate our differences. I find that when we celebrate our differences, we learn from each other. We get excited and often want to explore something that is unique to someone else. I believe in unity consciousness. I will continue to devote my life to helping each of us find our common humanity.

- In conversation with a few trusted friends, explore what you have in common and a few interesting differences.

Servant Leaders

July 31st

"A man was hiking in the woods when he saw a deer that had lost his leg, and he wondered how it would continue to survive. He decided to watch a while when he noticed the mountain lion with game in its mouth. When the lion had eaten his share, he left the rest of the meal for the deer. The next day, the man noticed Spirit fed the deer yet again by means of the lion. He thought to himself, *if Spirit provides for this deer, then, by all means, it will take care of all my needs as well.* He put his trust in the Lord and waited to be provided for, just as the deer had done without question. After a couple of days and weeks during which nothing was provided and now literally starving to death, the man heard a voice,

"Open your eyes to the Truth. *Be* the lion and stop following the way of the injured deer."

- Terry Cole-Whittaker, *The Inner Path from Where You Are to Where You Want to Be*

I believe we are called to be servant leaders. When we serve others, we, and everyone we serve, grow and flourish. We are all capable of empathy, courage, and sacrifice. Empathy and trust must become our highest standards for our work and our life. To earn trust, we must extend trust, and believe in the goodness of people. We must lead with the balance of heart and mind. When we work from a servant leadership mindset, we tap into our spiritual well-being. We have a more expanded view of the possibilities of life. Our work as servant leaders leaves us feeling inspired, satisfied, fulfilled and grateful. All those we serve, are someone's beloved child and we as servant leaders, are responsible for their lives. We need to rebuild our world; our highest priority is the care and compassion of all.

♦ How can you support the needs of others through a servant leadership mindset?

August

"How far you go in life depends on your being tender with the young, compassionate, with the aged, sympathetic, with the striving, and tolerant of the weak, and the strong. Because someday in life, you will have been all of these."

~ George Washington Carver

Serve Others

August 1st

I find that to retain or build my belief in myself,
it is important to help others build their belief in themselves.

If you wish to experience joy,
help others experience joy.

If you wish to experience acceptance,
then be accepting of those that are different than you.

If you wish to feel forgiveness,
then be forgiving.

If you wish to feel safe and secure,
then help others to be safe and secure.

If you want to feel valued,
then help others to be valued.

If you want to experience friendship,
then be a good friend.

If you want to be at peace,
then help others find peace.

If you want to be loved,
then give love.

Whatever we want for ourselves,
we must help others find the same.

♦ Reflect on what you want in your life at this time. Once you have identified that desire, find someone you can give that desire to.

Our Highest Self

August 2nd

Everyone needs recognition of who they really are on the highest level. When we see the world from the perspective of our highest self, we radiate connection, positivity, and unconditional love.

We heal the feeling of separation and exclusion.

> "There is a divine spark in everyone, no matter how dim."
> - God speaking in the television show "Joan of Arcadia"

♦ In conversation with a trusted friend, share with each other how you see each other in the best light.

Choose Lovingness

August 3rd

Lovingness is an attitude. It transforms our vision and experience of the world. We focus on gratitude and forgiveness, rather than being right. We express love by acknowledging contributions others have brought into our lives.

Love is the way of being.

Love is the way we relate to life.

♦ Identify three people in your life who have made many contributions. Find a way to express your gratitude for what they have brought into your life.

The Cause of Love

August 4th

In all the great literature (poetry, prose, plays, novels, fiction, non- fiction) of the world there are countless references to love.

There are few pieces of writing that celebrate logic.

"Logic never attracts men to the point of carrying them away."
- Alexis Carrell

Love excites passion, warms our heart, and softens our walls. Given the transformational nature of love, why do we base so many of our decisions on logic? Maybe we fear that we will be disrespected if we don't show how logical we are.

I want to be respected; but I also want to be carried away, transformed, totally used up in the cause of love.

◆ When was the last time you were carried away, transformed by a piece of music, poem, story, movie, or other form of art?

Friends

August 5th

Friends are those people with whom we speak with love and passion without being filled with fear, doubt, or even the need for approval.

I am blessed with deep, abiding friendships in my life. They are an oasis when my life has been dry and cracked with my own intensity. They have been a cool and refreshing drink of clean, clear water when my heart was burned from its loving passions. When I was ill and alone, one visited and sat with me, even when I could not remember his presence. Another was always there, by my side, providing kinship and camaraderie. Others ensured my freedom as I explored the mysteries of my existence. Many others waited patiently as I searched for truth in creative adventures that led me back to their trusted friendship. I have prayed in my "dark nights of the soul" waiting to hear God's voice.

Honest, loving friends are parts of your soul. They soften the harshness of the world.

Friendship in ancient German means "place of high safety".

This safety, this friendship, opens us to God.

"My friends are the beings through whom God loves me."
- St. Martin

◆ In conversation with a trusted friend, share your feelings of emotional safety in their presence.

Love Ripples

August 6th

Our spiritual development is the most important process of our lives.

When we grow spiritually, everyone around us is uplifted and enhanced. Love radiates like ripples in a pond. Everyone around us is positively influenced by kindness, compassion, empathy, and love. Forgiveness and gratitude benefit everyone. Every action, every word, every thought, is recovered in the energy of the universe and returns to the sender.

Every kindness last forever.

- What aspect of your spiritual development is calling to you?

The Essential Question

August 7th

The challenges of life have moved me to dislike small talk. I am only interested in what is essential. In the past, my focus and authenticity have frightened some people. Now in my 70 plus years, I ask what is essential and others seem drawn to the essence of my question. They see the light through the conversation.

The dialogue of what is essential is how we learn and love each other. We are transformed through the story of connection and compassion.

I am blessed to share my life with Sandra. I am in awe of her compassion, empathy, caring, and courage. As she sits by our daughter's bedside in intensive care, I am humbled by her unconditional love. I thank God every day for the grace and blessing that is Sandra. Everyone she touches is enhanced.

♦ Who are the people in your life that enhance your well-being. Let them know.

Angel

August 8th

My beloved daughter Ashley is labeled "developmentally delayed". Over 39 years ago at the Children's Hospital in Philadelphia, the medical diagnosis was "severely, profoundly, retarded". Ashley has the physical abilities of a 2-month-old infant. She looks to me to be about 10 years old. She cannot speak, she cannot consciously move her body. She is tube fed. She is either in her pink wheelchair, or in her bed. She averages 4 seizures a day, and that is a good day.

Ashley is my role model. She is pure, innocent, she has no defenses. She cannot say no, don't do that to me, she cannot raise her arm to protect herself. She can love. She can emulate love like an angel. She is a gift from God. One of my favorite things to do is pray and meditate with Ashley. I find peace in her unconditionally loving presence.

It is because Ashley is so challenged and vulnerable, I have learned to openly share my challenges and vulnerability. I reveal my own imperfections and share my fragilities without shame.

Ashley draws people to her. They approach with curiosity, gentleness, and genuine caring and affection. She has an innate wisdom that emanates from her as a loving, welcoming, spiritual presence. Her life has been a life of loving and being loved. Ashley may be delayed developmentally, but she is advanced spiritually.

I find deep peace seeing the world through her innocent eyes.

♦ Who are the special souls in your life who emanate unconditional love? Let them know how much you appreciate them.

Practice

August 9th

"To love someone is to strive to accept that person exactly the way he or she is, right here and now."
- Fred Rogers, *The World According to Mister Rogers: Important Things to Remember*

Our life experience is a limitless journey of practice and progress, not perfection. We are all in a relationship in this journey of making mistakes and learning. We all have different life learning styles, and we all learn our life lessons at different rates of speed. We all must remember each of us is doing the best we can with what we know at the moment.

I seek to lovingly accept you as you are in that moment- even though you may be different than me, and hard for me to understand. It would be easier for me if you were like me, but it would be far less interesting and neither of us would grow or learn anything new.

Our relationships along life's journey allow us to keep practicing.

Practice, practice, practice.
Progress, progress, progress.
Improvement, improvement, improvement.

- Where are you currently improving?
- Where do you still need to improve?

Love is Life

August 10th

Love is knowing we are connected to everything.

Imagine what a wonderful world it would be if we could walk into every interaction with loving intention. Love often brings forth a similar response. Both the giver of love and the receiver of love benefit. Research into loving kindness tells us that the witness of loving interaction also benefits. Love is also healing.

I've witnessed and felt it whenever our daughter Ashley is in the hospital. The love of her family, friends, nurses, and doctors is a part of her healing process.

Our world needs your love. Love brings value and worth into our relationships. Love brings appreciation, joy, compassion, empathy, connection, celebration, and life. Love connects us to meaning and purpose in our life. Love helps us see the good in others. Love also helps us appreciate our unique selves. Love helps us appreciate rather than judge.

Love is life.

- What are the strongest loving connections in your life? Offer these individuals your love today.

Relationships

August 11th

Relationships allow us to know everything at a deeper level. Through relationships, we learn more about ourselves. We learn more about each other. We learn more about our future. We learn more about what we believe.

All relationships start with two separate, distinct lives. We must first be ourselves before we can be in a relationship with anyone. Our first task in building a strong and healthy relationship is to build a strong and healthy self. This is the essential healing. We must honor ourselves before we know how to honor another.

- How are you honoring yourself today?

Teach

August 12th

Teach respect by showing and modeling respect to students.

Establish healthy communication patterns. Put the emphasis on listening. Remember, we have two ears and only one mouth. We need to listen at least 50% more. Often listening is the only assistance a child needs to help them solve a problem.

Teach trustworthiness as a core human value and an essential ingredient in character development.

Promote the behavior of responsibility. Remind students that they are 100% responsible for what they think, feel, say, and do. No one can make you think, feel, say, or do anything.

Demonstrate moral character. Establish ground rules in the classroom. Teach a true sense of right and wrong.

Promote helping others and a service mentality. Assign yourself, don't wait. Encourage cross age tutoring. If something needs to be done, do it! Democracy is not a spectator sport; get and stay involved.

Most importantly, teach students to acknowledge the existence of problems. Encourage them to seek help from parents, other teachers, and counselors when they have a concern.

- Sit in quiet reflection and remember all the students you have served.

Skills of Life

August 13th

Be who you really are. Be authentic, be of service. Affect in a positive way the lives of those you love and the lives of all you encounter. Assist in ending the suffering of others. We are all connected.

Our basic instinct is love.

Present yourself authentically to the world. Be true to yourself. Share your struggles in your process.

There is a practical way to eliminate violence. Simply detach from the need to judge and the belief in separation.

Dr. Karen Osterman reminds me in her research "the more I know about you, the less likely I am to even think of harming you."

We must close the human gap. We must become known. Focus on unity. We are more alike than we are different.

Speak your truth with kindness and compassion.

Practice integrity.

Work for the common good.

Practice gratitude.

Practice forgiveness.

Share what you have (gifts, talents, abundance, life).

Continued...

Balance personal and work life.

Love each other or at least do no harm.

Eat healthy.

Be your best self- stop comparison.

Focus on all your blessings.

Express love.

Pray and meditate.

Listen to the "still, small voice".

Every act is an act of self-definition.

- Inspired by the work of Neil Donald Walsch.

♦ Treat yourself to a reading of one of Neil Donald Walsch's books.

LifeSkills Conference Reflections

August 14th

Thank you to the LifeSkills Conference staff and students and all our Masonic sponsors. In the third week of July, we gathered at the Masonic Conference Center at Patton Campus of the Pennsylvania Masonic Village in Elizabethtown. We came together in our passion for respect, responsibility, and healthy relationships. We focused on servant leadership. We built a community of kindness, compassion, gratitude, and forgiveness. Each of us is a drop of water in an ocean of loving unity.

After six weeks of recovery from a spinal injury, I experienced the healing. I was humbled by the limitless dedication and commitment of our LifeSkills Conference staff. I was uplifted by the trust and open heartedness of all our participants. Differences were recognized, accepted, and celebrated. From this respect for differences, arose a unity of consciousness. We are of a Divine unity. We are all made of the same stuff. We are now aware of this greater spirit. Our fears are lessened. We know we are supported. In our moments together, we know we were made of love. We are blessed when we realize what we are made of and what we have risen from.

- With a trusted friend or colleague, share a healing experience.

Whole Child Educators: Stay True to the Calling

August 15th

As an educator, teacher, counselor, administrator, and now consultant, I always care about being effective. Am I getting through to my audience, to my listener, to my students?

As whole child educators, we need to remember to be faithful to our mission. We need to be grateful for the gifts that we share. We need to be grateful that the world needs our gifts. I experience a world where children, families, and colleagues need passionate and caring educators now, possibly more than ever before. We must never allow politics and testing to crush the spirits of the children and colleagues whom we cherish.

We must stay true to our calling. We must stay true to the precious children entrusted to our care. We know in our heart of hearts we will never accomplish our tasks in our lifetime. When at the end of the time we can say "I was true to my calling", we can leave with a full heart.

- Have you followed your calling?
- How do you feel about the path you have followed?
- Are there other roads you want to take?

A Symphony of Hearts and Souls

August 16th

We each have a unique gift to bring to the world. It is our own responsibility to develop and share this gift. The world will not be whole if we do not share our gifts and strengths. We create a safe atmosphere for our students to nurture, practice, and ultimately perform their gifts on life's stage.

We build a community that is safe, accepting, and celebrates differences. We create harmony in relationships and collaboration through problem- solving, effective communication, and creative thinking.

We conduct a symphony of hearts and souls sharing the music of joy and grace. Our collective gifts create a synergy… and love is revealed.

- How are you building community throughout the school year?

A Community of Trust

August 17th

In our schools, we seek to create a healthy, trusting, emotionally safe community of learners. Community means that we are connected. We are open to relationship and connection. We are never completely alone. In our initiatives we create a community where joy and sharing become the norm. In our small groups we dialogue deeply and address concerns and challenges.

We create opportunities that invite our intellect. We analyze, offer logical solutions, and work through the methods of science.

We create a safe space that invites our emotions to be heard. We play, cry; we can be angry without hurting anyone. We are authentic; we are transparent; we are real.

We create solutions that recognize perseverance as one of the most essential human traits. In teams, we consolidate the effort and energy to reach shared goals.

In our community of trust, we all grow into servant leaders. Through our principles and practice of respect for self and others, we grow as leaders. We are responsible for all we think, feel, say, and do. We are responsible for forming quality relationships.

- What are the primary ingredients in creating a trusting community in your classroom and your school?

Empathy in Conversation

August 18th

Our challenge continues to be finding a way to deep, meaningful conversation.

"Around 10 billion text messages were sent globally in 2012, but how many of them involved conversations that inspired, consoled, or touched people?"
- Roman Krznaric, *Empathy: Why It Matters, and How to Get It*

Our LifeSkills Conference is dedicated to deep, meaningful conversation. We challenge ourselves and each other to be vulnerable, authentic, and transparent. Through activity, as well as small and large group conversation, we explore the deep and sensitive aspects of being human. Our empathy and courage take us to new territories in human trust. We slow down and become attuned to the needs of others. Our empathy is built on mutuality. We risk being open with others and they, in turn, feel safe to open up to us.

"The antidote to shame is empathy… if we can share our story with someone who responds with empathy and understanding, shame can't survive."
- Dr. Brené Brown, *Daring Greatly: How the Courage to Be Vulnerable Transforms the Way We Live, Love, Parent, and Lead*

We must be kind and gentle with ourselves and joined together in compassionate community.

♦ How can you create an atmosphere of emotional safety so students can share their story with you?

Lessons

August 19th

As I reflect on our Masonic LifeSkills Conference, I appreciate that we ask young adults essential life questions.

We begin with "Who Are You?" and "Why Are You Here?" These questions ask us all to go deeper to begin to focus on our life's mission. Our Masonic LifeSkills Conference focuses on the following lessons:

- Servant leadership is not an accomplishment; it is a way of life. It brings its own intrinsic rewards; what is essential is our intentions.
- As servant leadership increases, we become more attracted to love, peace, and beauty rather than in things or short-term gains.
- Forgiveness and gratitude become a habit.
- As we continue to be connected throughout the world, we become aware that as we improve in our private lives, the world improves with us. What we do to serve others automatically benefits everyone; we are all connected in this life.
- We can make a gift of our life by being kind, respectful, forgiving, responsible, compassionate, and integrous. We seek to offer these gifts at all times, in all places, to everyone including ourselves.
- Integrity is strong, constructive, practical, and simply "works". Our integrity comes from taking responsibility for what we think, feel, say, and do.
- We decide daily to "be kind to all life". To respect the sacredness of life. Dr. David Hawkins stated, "Simple kindness to oneself and all that lives is the most powerful, transformational force of all." The values of compassion, forgiveness, and understanding become prominent.

Continued...

- Out of all-inclusive, unconditional, loving compassion comes the growth and health of humanity.
- We support and focus on the solutions instead of attacking and judging the causes.
- Acceptance and understanding resolves strife, conflict, and pain.
- Gratitude is more powerful than retribution.
- Keeping focus on a goal inspires us to accomplish the goal; what is held in our hearts and minds becomes real.
- All we need to progress towards our goal is patience, faith, and the surrender of resistance.
- Courage is not the absence of fear, but the willingness to move through it. We reach out to others, pushing through our fear of rejection, failure, and hurt.
- Each positive choice moves us closer to additional choices. Every choice matters. Choose well.
- We recognize each other at our highest level. We see the same Self in everyone. This unity through community heals us of separation.
- Make a gift of your life. Share love, acceptance, and compassionate service. When we uplift others, everyone is uplifted in the process. Trust the process.
- There is no greater calling in life than to be of service to others.

♦ What students or staff members need us now?

Empowering Students to Succeed

August 20th

Respect, Responsibility, and Relationships. They are the essential three R's for success in life. Each moment a child lives is a new and unique moment in the world. A moment that never was before and will never be again. What do we teach our children in school? We teach them that 2+2=4 and that Washington, D.C. is the capitol of the United States.

We must also teach children of their capabilities. SEL helps them realize that they are capable of greatness, that they are beautiful, and that they can experience self-fulfillment through service to others. We teach children that they are unique. We tell them they are a marvel of creation. In the entire world, there is no other person like them. We teach them to respect themselves and others. We teach them to respect diversity and welcome and appreciate differences. We teach them that responsibility and service are the rents we pay for the privilege of being alive and blessed in America. We spend significant time on what it means to be a healthy person. We describe healthy relationships as those that contribute to the overall good of our society. We help our students set goals to make a positive impact back home in their schools, youth groups, houses of worship, and families. We ask students to stand up for values that enhance the world, such as respect, responsibility, and service to others.

"Each time a person stands up for an idea, or acts to improve the lot of others, or strikes out against injustice, s(he) sends forth a tiny ripple of hope…those ripples build a current that can sweep down the mightiest walls of oppression and resistance."
- Robert F. Kennedy

♦ Reflect on all the essential human skills you teach your students daily.

Be True to Yourself

August 21st

Be true to yourself. Not the self that is imposed by your family, not the self they imagined you to be, but your own true self. Your true self has been carved by our invisible father and has been nurtured in the womb of your unseen mother. Your true self is made in the image and likeliness of God.

When you are true to yourself, you honor God within you. When you are true to yourself, you respond to God, "Thank you for my divine purpose." Not the purpose of others, not the path of anyone else, but of the fulfilling of your unique calling.

Be true to yourself. Express your God-given talents with the knowing that no one can deliver your gift to the world. Do not abdicate. There is no one who can duplicate the inner fire of your heart. Only you hold the blueprint to God's plan for your success.

You may no longer stand on the sidelines. Others have gone before you. The hero's path is well worn. Now it is your time. SHINE!

It is your moment. Return to your center. Be the authentic power that God blessed you with. Be thankful for your purpose; be true to yourself. No one can express you. The world waits with ecstatic anticipation for your voice.

- What do you want to say?
- What do you want to do?
- What is holding you back?

Invisible Human Bond

August 22nd

I find something of myself in everyone I meet. Some of the qualities I find are warm and loving. Some of the qualities I would rather not recognize. I believe something passes between each of us and we share an invisible human bond.

Namaste.

I bow to the God in you that is the God in me. Let us begin a search for the God in everyone.

As we acknowledge the unconditional love in ourselves, let us also acknowledge the unconditional love in everyone we meet. There is a great unity in life.

Let us each clean our own front door with kindness, empathy, and compassion.

- What are some of your qualities that you see in others?

Love the Shadow

August 23rd

"Perhaps everything that frightens us, is, in its deepest essence, something helpless that wants our love.
- Rilke, *Letters to a Young Poet*

The only answer is love- love for the shadow and darkness within each of us. As we own our darkness, we rejoice in our own light. We each cry out for love. The only sane and satisfactory response to the challenges of life is love.

- What frightens you?
- How is this fear calling out for love?

I'll Meet You There

August 24th

"Out beyond ideas of wrongdoing and right doing, there is a field. I'll meet you there."
- Rumi

Take some time to explore divine acceptance in place of our ego's need to be right or wrong. Focus on the eternal, the unfolding of your spiritual growth. Give thanks for your past challenges. Value the learning and growth. Look forward to your evolving self.

- What new lessons and growth edges are you currently exploring?

The Powerful Impact of Kindness

August 25th

Simple human kindness is one of the greatest gifts of this life. It is a powerful, transformational process that can move the hardest heart. Kindness has no negativity, it uplifts, creates smiles, offers new perspectives, and always brings comfort. True and powerful kindness does not seek selfish reward.

It enhances the well-being of all involved. Scientific research has shown that serotonin levels are increased for both the giver and the receiver of kindness. Acts of kindness also raise the serotonin levels of those who witness the act of kindness. Serotonin is a natural chemical in the body that leads to increased happiness and the ability to react well to stress.

The effect of subtle, gentle, kindness has far-reaching, rippling effects.

- Reflect on one of the most recent kind acts that you received. Be aware of how you felt.
- What actions did you take after this act of kindness was bestowed upon you?

Kindness is Always Possible

August 26th

"Be kind whenever possible. It is always possible."
- His Holiness the Dalai Lama

I have the privilege to live with and to be married to Sandra, my role model of kindness. Her daily existence is bringing comfort and kindness to everyone with whom she comes into contact. Her life is an example that kindness is always possible.

♦ Be kind. Now.

To Be Loved

August 27th

"You do not need to do anything to be loved.
You do not have to perform or achieve,
or earn a merit badge or be witnessed doing good."
- Mark Nepo, *The Book of Awakening: Having the Life You Want by Being Present to the Life You Have*

It has taken me 70 years to learn, know, and believe this. It is my life's Work. It is today's work. We have all received messages to the contrary, which are old, deep wounds.

In my heart, where God's spirit and unconditional love is alive and well, it does not matter what I accomplish. It only matters how deeply I tried. Out of my trying comes sincerity, integrity, and love.

- Where are you making your best effort?

Friendship

August 28th

There is no real friendship until we share the personal experience of who we are. We cannot have both truth and love in our lives until we share our truth and love, until we speak from "I" and take responsibility. We must stop putting all our pain on "you", on the others in our lives. Until I take responsibility for my own mistakes, where I have stumbled and fallen, where I hurt and stop blaming my pain on others, I cannot know truth or love.

I have a friend. We have known each other for over 50 years. We have known each other across the continent. We have stood together in storms, never knowing if we would be safe. We have comforted each other through accidents, illness, fear, and loss. We have held each other when our parents died. I have loved him when he tried to hide, and my words could not reach him. He has loved me when I felt unworthy of love. Because we dared to trust, to open our souls to each other, because we have broken into pieces in front of each other, we have the privilege of saying, as if for the first time,

"You are my friend."

I look at him, after what for many is a lifetime, and say, "Tell me your truth. Share your love." Let us sit closely together, more interested in huddling together than flying away. Having a real friend, one with whom you can share your deepest fears and greatest joy, is a form of wealth that will bring you everything you need. To find this kind of friend, we must be this kind of friend.

♦ In conversation with a dear and trusted friend, share your appreciation and gratitude for your friendship.

Spreading Light

August 29th

"There are two ways of spreading light:
to be the candle or the mirror that reflects it."
- Edith Wharton

Sometimes in life, we get to be the candle, the source the light. We are inspired by some great deal or purpose, and we act, bringing our light into the world. More often, we are the mirror that reflects the light. We are part of a team, supporting a vision, playing an essential role, humbly contributing, being of service.

We are all connected to the light.

- How are you spreading the light?

Appreciation

August 30th

"The deepest principle of human nature
is the craving to be appreciated."
- William James, *The Principles of Psychology*

Today, extend value to everyone you meet. Who provides service to you? Who is your school custodian? Who cleans up after all of us are gone? Who began work today in the early morning so you could have lunch? Who warmed the bus before dawn so you could ride to school?

All of those in service deserve your care, attention, and appreciation.

♦ Reach out to anyone on the school staff who makes your life easier. Show them how much you appreciate them.

Authenticity

August 31st

Being authentic, being real, being your true self has more power than persuasion, debate, or force of will. Being authentic (who we truly are) connects us to the extra ordinary. Authenticity affects everyone we meet.

By being ourselves, we create an atmosphere of warmth for everyone. Our warmth emanates in all directions and, like the sun, causes everyone to grow. We are all emanations of loving compassion.

By being authentic, we experience life in all its vitality. Our authenticity and vulnerability innocently affect others and helps them to be more authentic. Through this emotional safety, we each grow and blossom in the light of unity.

- When are you most authentic?

Responsible Decision Making

September and October

Responsible Decision Making is similar to the scientific method. We are curious and open minded, which helps us explain, understand, and create. We make decisions based on facts, data, and a well-informed analysis of the information. We are then identifying solutions and action. We can assess and evaluate our actions and reflect on our role in personal family and community health and well-being. We can use critical thinking skills to recognize the impact of our decisions and actions on personal, interpersonal, and communal lives.

September

"A rock pile ceases to be a rock pile the moment man contemplates it, bearing within him the image of a cathedral."
~ Antoine de Saint-Exupery, Flight to Arras

There is Always a Choice

September 1st

"We cannot eliminate hunger, but we can feed each other. We cannot eliminate loneliness, but we can hold each other. We cannot eliminate pain, but we can live a life of compassion."
- Mark Nepo, *The Book of Awakening: Having the Life You Want by Being Present to the Life You Have*

We are not powerful enough to change the world. We can change our attitudes and behavior. We can choose to be kind, loving and compassionate. We are responsible for everything we think feel, say, and do. We live in an experience of endless choices. As long as we live, we can choose again. We can choose to comfort the uncomfortable, express our feelings, release the joy within our life, give and receive love. There is always a choice.

♦ Please share a choice you made this past week that was focused on compassion.

What Makes Schools Great is Being Human

September 2nd

The secret to a successful teaching and learning experience is relationship. Do we care? Are we connected? Is what I'm teaching meaningful and relevant to my students lives?

What is essential in school and life is how we treat people.

How do we treat our students?
How do we treat our co-workers?
How do we treat our administrators?
How do we treat our custodians?
How do we treat our aides?
How do we treat our bus drivers?
How do we treat our cafeteria workers?
How are we showing value to everyone we encounter?
How are we showing kindness, compassion, and gratitude?

What makes schools great is being human.

We must acknowledge people for what they do and most importantly, for who they are.

◆ Who will you acknowledge this week for the humanity they bring to your school?

Building a School Community

September 3rd

School Community Requirements

A community is a place where everyone works together for a common goal. To have a community, you need to have three things happening in your school:

- Respect- for self and others
- Responsibility- for yourself and that of your group
- Relationships- the ability to work collaboratively in a group and set aside your differences

Connecting the Community and Education

Every school, like every community, has its own distinct culture, values, and rules. By building a community in the school, teachers create a common feeling connected to others. For children to participate in a school community, to relate positively to others and become successful learners, their basic needs for sustenance, safety, and belonging must be met. Only after basic needs are met can human beings learn more.

- *Physiological needs*- the most basic needs of living creatures. Children who are hungry think about their bellies instead of learning.
- *Safety*- the feeling of security, comfort, and freedom from danger. When teachers create a safe classroom community, children can positively relate to others, explore their environment, and engage in learning.
- *Belonging*- the feeling of being accepted and loved. To seek acceptance and love from adults, children often exhibit behavior that tests acceptance. These children need adults who can create a school environment where everyone feels accepted and valued.

Continued...

- *Self-esteem*- the sense of one's own worth. Children who feel competent as learners are more open to new experiences, better able to empathize with others, and more willing to persevere in learning tasks than are children who are consistently feeling inadequate.

How to Get Your School Started
Discuss with your students the characteristics of a team. Have a team building vocabulary word of the day or week, such as respect, responsibility, cooperation, dependability, loyalty, etc. Build lessons and activities. Divide your class into small groups of teams. Assign specific duties to each member. Have the group come up with a team name, symbol, logo, mascot, etc. Integrate team building activities into your curriculum.

- Work on a math problem as a team
- Work on a science or social studies project as a group
- Write a story about their team
- Read a story as a team using buddy reading; and then present the story in a play form to the rest of the class
- Design a poster with a team name/self-portrait of each member
- Design and decorate a classroom bulletin board

For the first week or so of school, have a "question of the day" which would be a daily question that students would answer about themselves. If time is an issue, have them pair and share their responses with a different partner each day.

◆ Identify and implement one thing you will do this week to build a healthy classroom community.

Servant Leadership

September 4th

"If your actions inspire others to dream more, learn more, do more and become more, you are a leader."
- John Quincy Adams

Servant leadership does not mean power over others. Servant leadership is learning about our own unique, internal power. We must learn how to monitor our own strengths and weaknesses. We are at our best when we model the behavior we want to see in others.

Everyone wants and needs to feel safe. Leaders are responsible for creating and maintaining an emotionally and physically safe environment. That begins with developing relationships and working on trust. When leaders are trusted, both personal and professional growth is nurtured.

Servant leaders are aware that our own authenticity and vulnerability are strengths. Through behavior, we encourage owners to share their authenticity and vulnerability.

◆ Who is one of the most authentic and vulnerable people you know? Let them know you see their courage.

Building a School Family

September 5th

Schools can change the lives of children; and together, educators and children can change the world.

We must "fully embrace the responsibility
of the lives entrusted to us."
- Bob Chapman

Every school and school leader has the responsibility to create a school family and community that keeps children physically and emotionally safe. We must teach and model caring, forgiveness, gratitude, empathy, compassion, trust, respect, nurturing, and love. When we hold ourselves and children accountable, this is an act of love.

We need to treat each staff member and each student the way we want our own precious children to be treated.

We need to build a school family and community where everyone wants to come every day, where they will be nourished in mind, body, and soul.

We need to find role models and mentors for ourselves, our staff, our parents, and our students, mentors that model the essential social and emotional skills for being a good human being.

We need to see the potential in everyone in our school family. We need to encourage and inspire our staff and students to develop their strengths and passion.

We need to respect our talents, similarities, challenges, and differences. We need to celebrate our diversity as a school family. We need to support each other in our diversity.

Continued...

We need to be patient with those who are in pain and afraid of growth and change. We need to listen to their story and find out what has happened to them.

We need to help staff and students grow beyond our school family. Just like great, loving parents, we need to give them roots and ways to grow. At some point, they will all leave us, and we will know we have served them well.

We need to be real, authentic, vulnerable, and courageous. We need to laugh together, cry together, talk it out, talk it through, and forgive and forgive and forgive.

- How are you embracing the responsibility as an educational leader?

How Can We Transform Schools?

September 6th

How do we take standardized test oppressed educators and students to an experience where they are cared for and each of their lives matter?

We need to see everyone as a potential leader. We need to inspire and recognize their passion, heart, commitment, and compassion. We need to acknowledge the humanity and goodness in our school. I have found that if we take care of those we work with, they will take care of the work of teaching and learning. If we let people know we genuinely care about them, they will let others know they care. *Trust is the core of successful school transformation. We must give trust, to get trust.*

> "They found one variable that had great explanatory power: they called it "relational trust," which I read as a synonym of community. If a school had high relational trust and/or a leadership core that worked on trust building, that school had roughly a five out of seven chance of serving students better by the end of the decade."
>
> \- Parker Palmer, Arthur Zajonc, Megan Scribner,
> *The Heart of Higher Education: A Call to Renewal*

The children, caregivers, and educators of our nation are starving for positivity and authentic leadership in schools. Everyone I meet in education is passionate to show their love for children and their love of learning. Long-term, meaningful change is not easy and not fast. We need to make a heartfelt, soul-level commitment to do what is needed. Doing what is most human; taking care of each other.

- As an educator, in what ways are you most human?
- How is your humanity an asset in the school environment?

Mentoring

September 7th

Since my career as an educator and human services professional began at age 20, I have always been blessed to work with people younger than I am. In the past 50 years, I have worked with talented, passionate people who are often younger in years but not in wisdom. Wisdom for me has never been at the top of the graduate school hierarchy. It has always been in the heart, soul, and body of each individual life story.

I find joy in connecting young and old- in finding answers to social and educational challenges. The energy is abundant and effervescent. I believe we need to join to address our shared responsibility for the future. Together, we are the future. We are *our* future.

I love mentoring young adults. Mentoring is a two-way street. This mentality allows us to inspire the best in each other. I love helping people find their voice. There is great reward and meaning in sharing the authenticity and vulnerability of our voice. As mentors, we have the honor and privilege to create a safe and emotional space for a young voice to blossom and feel its truth.

In young voices are sounds of hope. We need the sound of hope, now! I am inspired by youthful voices. I am inspired by hope. We need to be inspired, now!

We must knock down all our perceived walls of difference and meet in a safe, emotional space. From this safe space, we will create wisdom.

♦ How are you empowering student voice in your school system?

Educational Leadership

September 8th

"What, if anything, about the way people are leading today needs to change in order for leaders to be successful in a complex, rapidly, changing environment where we're faced with seemingly intractable challenges and an insatiable demand for innovation?"
- Dr. Brené Brown, *Dare to Lead: Brave Work. Tough Conversations. Whole Hearts.*

I have the privilege to work with outstanding educational leaders throughout the United States. As I interact with superintendents, principals, and teacher leaders, I find that many of them have the skills needed to deal with today's challenges. One dear friend, a principal whom I admire greatly, refers to herself as the "lead learner" in her school. What a wonderful awareness. We are all lifetime learners. Either we are busy learning, or we are busy dying. The willingness to learn, to grow and be vulnerable, including, being able to admit "I don't know the answer, but let's work together to find it."

I find that the educational leaders I love working with are courageous. They are deeply committed to the growth and well-being of everyone for whom they care for and lead.

I also find that courage being modeled when educational leaders tell their story. When we tell our story, we empower others to do the same. We realize we are not the only one. We realize we are not alone. We are connected by our common humanity.

- *Educational leaders* acknowledge, affirm, and celebrate the hard work of the educators who devote their lives to children.
- *Educational leaders* have the courage and skill to give specific, descriptive, observable feedback to those they lead.

Continued...

- *Educational leaders speak their truth.* When new agendas and mandates with short timelines erupt, they speak to the fears and challenges that they and their staff feel.
- *Educational leaders model trust.* They work at building relationships and building community. They listen to different perspectives. They seek to understand and work towards empathy. "Trust profoundly impacts performance by providing the foundation for effective teamwork and intrinsic motivation." Dr. Paul Zak, *The Trust Factor: The Science of Creating High-Performance Companies*
- *Educational leaders show value and appreciation to everyone on their staff.* As one dear friend, who is a superintendent once said, "We love our staff and students when we hold them accountable."
- *Educational leaders welcome diversity. They celebrate inclusion.* They understand having hard conversations about differences enriches our community and builds everyone's trust.
- *Educational leaders take responsibility when something goes wrong and make every effort to make it right.*

As I continue to assess myself daily to continue to learn from all educational leaders I am blessed to work with, I find that I need to continue to find the courage to be vulnerable and speak my truth and listen to your truth. I need to remain true to my core values of love and commitment. I need to continue to trust and forgive when trust is broken and trust again.

- ♦ What new challenges are you rising to meet?
- ♦ How do your core values and commitment help you rise to meet challenge?

Safe Schools

September 9th

Educators must create a safe physical and emotional environment that allows our learners to explore the worlds of knowledge, compassion, understanding and empathy.

We all need an environment where we can be authentic and vulnerable. We all need a place to breathe, relax, and appreciate.

Many of our students bring a backpack of pain and past trauma into our schools. We cannot fix their past, but we can and must create safe and welcoming classrooms and schools. We can create a community where students feel they are cared for and loved. When we create a safe learning community, children heal, relax, and learn.

- How are you reaching out and including students who feel disconnected?

Perseverance

September 10th

So much of our focus in education continues to be teaching and celebrating the intellect.

In 1997, Dr. Paul Stoltz introduced the concept of Adversity Quotient. AQ, according to Stoltz, is a valid predictor of performance, ability to deal with stress and challenge, resilience, pressure, and health. Those of us with a high AQ can withstand significant adversity, maintain perspective, stay flexible and creative, enhanced self-esteem in the face of challenge and use adversity to move forward.
- Adapted from Stephen Cope, *Soul Friends*

Perseverance is one of the highest valued and most admired characteristics. Some of my perseverance role models are Viktor Frankl, Bob Wieland, Abraham Lincoln, Nelson Mandela, and Sandra and Ashley Stecher. One of the keys to perseverance is a belief in something greater than you, a higher calling, a greater sense of purpose, coupled with love and deep commitment to relationship. I have seen the perseverance, fueled by unconditional love, as Sandra has cared for Ashley these past 39 years. Due to undiagnosed learning differences in her youth, my wife Sandra does not think of herself as "smart". She is the most brilliant socially and emotionally intelligent person I know.

Her ability to persevere and be lovingly resilient is world class. My life, my work, our family, and many others are dependent on her social emotional intelligence, perseverance, and unconditional love.

♦ How has perseverance played a part in your health and success?

Human Rights

September 11th

Human rights begin in our individual hearts and minds.

Human rights are in the decisions and choices I make daily. Human rights begin in my home- how I treat my wife, and how I care for our special needs daughter. Human rights are in the conscious words of love and respect I choose to use to use with those that are closest to me.

Human rights are in my neighborhood- my choice to smile and say hello to everyone who passes me on my walk, my choice to engage with the people at the grocery store, my willingness to listen to the thoughts and feelings of all who enter my home and office.

Human rights are in every connection, interaction, speech, class, and workshop I offer to educators. Human rights are in my inclusion, acceptance, and respect of all differences.

Human rights are in my honoring the legacy of all those who have served our nation and our world, for all the lives given to bring peace and understanding to this planet.

Human rights are in my working for equality, justice, opportunity, dignity, and respect for all life.

Our human brains are hardwired for empathy. Love and kindness are in our DNA. Through the practice of love, kindness, and empathy, we will give and receive human rights for all.

- How are you speaking up and showing up for the human rights of others?

Changing Myself

September 12th

"Yesterday I was clever, so I wanted to change the world.
Today I am wise, so I'm changing myself."
- Rumi

I work very hard at offering assistance rather than trying to change someone. I am sometimes tempted to want to change family, friends, workmates, and loved ones. When I am aware my helping is slipping into changing, I look in the mirror and ask, "What areas of my life need to be changed? What do I need to do to grow?" We all need to find our own joy. We all, as Joseph Campbell suggested, "need to find our own bliss".

When I attempt to try and change someone to be as I think they should be, we both are hurt. I have always found it is healthier when I accept someone as they are. Mother Teresa once said, "If everyone cleaned up their own doorstep, the whole world would be clean." I can only change myself. In each situation life presents to me, I realize if I want to change the situation, I must first change myself.

"To change ourselves effectively,
we first have to change our perceptions."
- Stephen R. Covey, *The 7 Habits of Highly Effective People*

When I see others in the world through the eyes of love, I see them as they truly are, Children of God. Seeing through the eyes of love changes our perspective, changes ourselves, and often changes others. When we feel acceptance, we can let our light shine.

◆ In conversation with a trusted friend, discuss the differences between offering assistance and trying to change someone.

Our Ability to Respond

September 13th

With knowledge comes responsibility.
With responsibility comes choice.
With choice, comes the future.

We have within us the capacity for knowledge and wisdom. To know, we need to ask, to explore, and practice. We gain wisdom as we use our knowledge. We learn responsibility as we put our wisdom (heart) and knowledge (intellect) into action.

The more responsible we are, the more choices life offers us. We are never given more than we can handle; even though there are times we don't believe we can handle some experiences. We learn we can respond to the increased challenges.

The goal of life shapes us, and our world, in such a way that love is extended to all humanity and to all life on the earth.

We can respond with love and transform our world.

- In conversation with a trusted friend, explore your thoughts on responsibility.

The Price of Being Authentic

September 14th

I have learned that no matter what vision I follow, there is always potential for conflict. When I have attempted to avoid all conflict, often to appease others, I have often hurt myself. In my past, when I've passionately worked to achieve my dreams, I have faced the disapproval of those who wanted me to stay the same.

The price of being authentic is that we will never be what everyone else wants us to be. I have found the greater cost is not being myself, not being real. When I am more concerned with not ruffling the status quo and trying to please others, something precious and vulnerable suffers deep inside me. Throughout the past ten years, I am aware that not being true to myself is destructive to my spirit.

I'm now at a place in my life that I pray to be authentic, vulnerable, and courageous. I am healthy when I am true to myself and resist the approval of others.

- How does seeking the approval of others damage our health and well-being?

Choice

September 15th

I have no choice in aging. I have no choice that our beloved daughter needed eye surgery. I have no choice about what someone else thinks or feels about me.

I have *total* choice on how I respond.

I can choose to respond to my aging knowing that the wisdom and experiences I have gathered will help others. I can respond to our daughter's eye surgery knowing she is in God's hands and that she will see this beautiful world again. No matter what other's think or feel about me, I can choose to share my truth, to be authentic, and to be a man of integrity.

I find it empowering to know that, in every moment, there is a choice. My choices are expressed as my life. When I connect to my spirit, I feel peace and calm in knowing I have chosen well. I am supported by the Divine. I am at peace.

- What choices bring you peace of mind?

Gifts

September 16th

Your gifts cannot reach maturity until they are used to SERVE the greater good.

I do not give lectures. I do not give courses.
I do not give charity. I give myself.
- Adapted from Walt Whitman

When we give ourselves, when we share from our sense of purpose, we go beyond the physical into the spiritual. This gift is enduring. It is indestructible. It is immeasurable. Weapons cannot destroy it, fire cannot burn it, water cannot drown it. It is timeless. We must strive to serve the welfare of the world. Our devotion to service will attain the goal of life.
Do you work with the welfare of others in mind?
- Adapted from Stephen Cope

- How are you giving of yourself in service to a greater good?
- What is your sense of purpose and how do you begin now?

Commitment

September 17th

"Until one is committed, there is hesitancy, the chance to draw back, always ineffectiveness. Concerning all acts of initiative (and creation), there is one elementary truth, the ignorance of which kills countless ideas and splendid plans: that the moment one definitely commits oneself, then Providence moves too. All sorts of things occur to help one that would never otherwise have occurred. A whole stream of events issues from the decision raising in ones favor all manner of unforeseen incidences and meetings and material assistance which no man could have dreamed would have come his way."
- W.H. Murray, *The Scottish Himalayan Expedition*

Life is built on a series of small course corrections- small choices that add up to something big- our lives. Your work is no longer your work.

It is The Work.
The Work is a path to Divinity.
Work and Worship are one.

"How we spend our days is how we spend our lives."
- Annie Dillard, *The Writing Life*

Give yourself entirely to the Work but let go of the outcome.

♦ If our life is built on a series of small course corrections, what have been those small course corrections in your life?

The Neuroscience of Optimism

September 18th

Dr. Andrew Newberg of Jefferson University Hospital shares in his book *How God Changes Your Brain: Breakthrough Findings from a Leading Neuroscientist*: "Hope, faith, and optimism are the best ways to exercise your brain."

Our inner critic (pessimist) resides in the right pre-frontal lobe of our brain. Our inner optimist resides in the left pre-frontal lobe of our brain. Research shows that people who consistently maintain hope and optimism are the happiest and most successful people in the world.

Which voice do you choose to listen to?

Barbara Fredrickson, one of the founders of Positive Psychology, recommends, "Every time you catch yourself having a negative feeling, focus on your attitude on three to five positive aspects of your life."

Begin with reviewing what went well today.

What did you do that helped others?
What are you grateful for?

The research shows if we do this for seven days, our self-esteem will grow for the following three months.

- ♦ Focus on 3-5 positive aspects of your life. Do this for seven days and check self-awareness and mental health.

Kindness

September 19th

Be kind and forgiving with no expectation of reward, knowing that one day someone will do the same for you.

- Just be kind.

Be Your Authentic Self

September 20th

Our life is a gift. What we make of our life is a gift back to our source. When we serve others in love, we lift ourselves and all those we serve. The ultimate gift is to be kind, forgiving, and compassionate in everything we do and say, including to ourselves.

"When Akiba was on his deathbed, he bemoaned to his rabbi that he felt he was a failure. His rabbi moved closer and asked why, and Akiba confessed that he had not lived a life like Moses. The poor man began to cry admitting that he feared God's judgment. At this, his rabbi leaned into his ear and whispered gently, God will not judge Akiba for not being Moses, God will judge Akiba for not being Akiba."

\- *The Talmud*

Our primary task in life is to be ourselves. The Universe is full of abundance. In each of us are God's unique lights. The infinite diversity of abundance does not ask us to compare, measure, or evaluate. Infinite love only asks that we be our authentic self. Each of us is perfect, just the way we are.

- How are you being fully authentic?

My Calling

September 21st

"The purpose of life is not to be happy. It is to be useful, to be honorable, to be compassionate, to have it make some difference that you have lived and lived well."
- Ralph Waldo Emerson

Recently I've spent time with family and friends who have retired. They lovingly ask if I am retired, and I respond no. I am now moving into the first year of my 70th decade of life. I have no desire to retire. One of the greatest blessings in my life is I get to do Work that I love. I feel on purpose. I feel I am fulfilling the mission God called me to accomplish. My Work brings me great joy. It moves me forward in my life. It brings meaning and purpose to each day.

What I do every day is mostly filled with joy. Even when it is hard, painful, and sometimes extremely stressful, below the surface, deeper than my ego, there is joy.

One aspect of my Work is to communicate a positive message of hope. It is my belief everyone can find joy in their work. All our work, all our lives, contribute to the creation of a beautiful world.

- What are your days full of?
- What would you like to change or add to your daily experience?

What Really Matters?

September 22nd

"What we do when our arm is raised, about to strike or soothe, will determine the next hundred years."
- Mark Nepo, *The Book of Awakening: Having the Life You Want by Being Present to the Life You Have*

"We are one gesture away from being the cruelty that we have suffered or one kindness from helping each other heal."
- Mark Nepo, *The Book of Awakening: Having the Life You Want by Being Present to the Life You Have*

We need to ask ourselves, *what really matters*? We need to ask each other *what is essential*? We then must lovingly challenge each other to live the answers. We must lean towards each other.

As we lean into each other, we create a support system that nurtures our common core beliefs. The common core beliefs of life and community have always held humankind together. Humanity always comes together in tragedy. Great loss brings great love.

Life teaches us to contribute to the good of the whole. In isolation, we die. In unity, we live.

In our human DNA, there is empathy, compassion, collaboration, and respect. These characteristics are essential to our humanity.

As we repair the world, we repair ourselves.
As we prepare our personal worlds, we repair our wounded world.

♦ In conversation with a friend or loved one, discuss what is essential in your life.

Integrity

September 23rd

The definition of integrity is… "Steadfast adherence to a moral code".

Integrity has its roots in the Latin *integritas,* from integer: whole-meaning, "the quality or condition of being whole or undivided; complete". Integrity is an ongoing, active lifelong practice of staying undivided in an effort to become whole.

My life has been blessed with many role models for integrity; my father, Reverend Dr. Martin Luther King Jr., Rosa Parks, Nelson Mandela, and Gandhi have all been men and women of courage who stood for the core values of integrity. Throughout my life and work, I've always tried to create circles of trust that allowed participants to build a community. In these classroom communities, we have participants develop a sense of authenticity and vulnerability.

Integrity builds trust. Research and education have proven that high relational trust and trust building allow schools to better serve students. (Bryk and Schneider, *Trust in Schools: A Core Resource for Improvement*).

Trust hold schools together and trust holds relationships together.

"Integrity is choosing courage over comfort;
it's choosing what is right over what is fun, fast, or easy;
and it's practicing your values, not just professing them."
- Dr. Brené Brown, *Braving the Wilderness:*
The Quest for True Belonging and the Courage to Stand Alone

- How are you building trust and integrity in your students?

Real Kindness Requires…

September 24th

"It takes courage to be kind."
- Maya Angelou

What can I do today to be kind? What small good can I offer my little corner of the world? Our hellos, thank you's, have a good day, and can I help you with that, are all micro kindnesses. Micro kindnesses are those daily, thoughtful actions that bring good into the world. Anything that supports human value, growth, health, and development, helps create a community of emotional safety and caring.

Kindness requires courage. There's nothing courageous about manipulation, lack of civility, or shutting down an opposing perspective. Real kindness requires strength, compassion, empathy, patience, and generosity of spirit.

We must conquer fear. Let us all pray and act to be courageous and kind and know that every micro kindness is an act of love.

- What are you standing up for in the lives of your students?

Be the First...

September 25th

The first to apologize,
creates courage.

The first to forgive,
creates understanding.

The first to forget,
creates happiness.

- Today be the first to apologize, understand, and forget.

Gratitude

September 26th

Simple acts of gratitude are healthy for the giver and the receiver.

Gratitude, like your daily exercise, relaxation, and good nutrition, needs to be practiced on a regular basis. Consistency brings health and wellness. Showing appreciation, creating a gratitude list, keeping a journal, and writing letters of thankfulness all have positive effects. They also help others "pay it forward".

There is no small gratitude. Simple thank you's for someone listening to you, preparing a meal, taking out the trash, cleaning up after us, helping with bags of groceries or books…all acts of gratitude are beneficial.

In our schools, we can model gratitude for our students by thanking them kindly for focusing their attention, following the rules, keeping each other physically and emotionally safe, being kind, including others in activities, helping with homework, and being quiet when needed. Gratitude will help our students repeat the positive behavior. Repeated positive behaviors, like gratitude, benefit everyone.

- How are you modeling gratitude for your students?

Forgive and Heal

September 27th

"The pain was necessary to know the truth,
but we don't have to keep the pain alive to keep the truth alive."
- Mark Nepo, *The Book of Awakening: Having the Life You Want by Being Present to the Life You Have*

It is not the better part of our wisdom to create our identity by our past hurts and pains. The more we hold on to our burning anger and resentment at those who have harmed us, the more our wounds stay open. We rationalize that we seek justice, fairness, and apology. We must reclaim our power. Stop waiting for something magical to come and heal us. We must heal ourselves.

When we forgive, we do not excuse the past hurtful behavior, with forgiveness comes our own healing. We must exchange resentment for inner freedom. When we let go and forgive, we can heal and live.

- How are you currently healing?
- Where do you need to let go and forgive?

Forgiveness Will Save Our Lives

September 28th

"Don't let your history dictate your destiny."
- Bishop T.D. Jakes

Don't let the pain of past mistakes or disagreements spoil your present experience. When we dig up old resentments, we put ourselves in the role of victim.

All of life is a learning experience. There's always an opportunity to see the light or the darkness. Happiness is a choice. There are always blessings along with our pain. When we feel uncomfortable, angry, or hurt about something in the past, we are re-living a memory. We are choosing to live in the past and recreate hurt and disappointment. Choose to move forward. Rejoice in the present. Follow the still, small voice. Let go and let God.

Love is the only sane and satisfying response to the challenges of life. Authenticity and vulnerability remove obstacles. My daily work is gratitude and forgiveness.

When I focus on gratitude, it is impossible to be unhappy. Forgiveness offers love to others and offers life and love to us.

Forgiveness will save our lives. Gratitude focuses on the good. Forgiveness and focusing on love, brings connection, creativity, and joy.

♦ Reflect on how forgiveness and gratitude have enhanced your life.

Forgiveness Sets Us Free

September 29th

"Forgiveness is the fragrance of the violet
which still clings to the heel that crushed it."
- George Roemisch

Forgiveness is one of the essential human, social, emotional skills. In my experience, it includes humility and acceptance of my very human frailties. I'm aware of my ability to make a mistake and I need to remember who those who have hurt me, are also human and make mistakes.

As I learn and practice forgiveness, I offer understanding and freedom to those that have injured me, and I offer freedom to myself.

"To forgive is to set a prisoner free and
discover that the prisoner was you."
- Lewis B. Smedes, *Forgive and Forget:
Healing the Hurts We Don't Deserve*

Forgiveness sets us free and accepts the situation that happened to let go of past hurt and anger. Forgiveness sets us free to focus on our future, our dreams, and our passions.

I pray that my behavior is consistent with my core values of love, compassion, empathy, and integrity. I want to continue to live my life on purpose, serving God and the children and educators of our schools. I want to continue bringing down walls and building bridges.

◆ In quiet reflection, focus on the bridges you have built throughout your life.

You Are Irreplaceable

September 30th

"No one can really know what you are called to or what you are capable of, but you. Even if no one sees or understands, you are irreplaceable."
- Mark Nepo, *Finding Inner Courage*

Every summer, the Pennsylvania Masonic Youth Foundation brings children ages 12-17 to the Patton Campus in Elizabethtown, PA, to experience what they are capable of. Through a series of social, emotional, mental, and physical challenges, we invite over 100 students and 30 staff to explore leadership from the inside out. Through safe, and supportive developmentally appropriate groups (teams), we explore our capabilities, significance, and worthiness.

Some students arrive cautious and tentative and leave empowered, knowing that they are capable of greatness. They leave with written plans of action defining how they will be servant leaders to their schools, communities, houses of worship, organizations, and families.

The Pennsylvania Masonic Youth Foundation through the LifeSkills Conference is positively impacting school organizations, school buildings, and school districts. The LifeSkills staff and participants return to their schools and help them understand the integration of social emotional learning with academic achievement.

The essence of our work in the Pennsylvania Masonic LifeSkills Conference is to create caring and compassionate young people- change agents who understand that leadership is not about accolades, but all about helping all to achieve. An essential ingredient in that achievement is the service we *must* provide to our communities and fellow human beings. As we serve others, we improve.

Continued...

Our prosperity is not only measured in acquisitions and bank statements. Our prosperity is also measured in the joy of making our world a bit better because of our contribution. Kind-heartedness and genuine concern for the welfare of others is our life's work. Every step forward in service and leadership benefits everyone.

- How are you helping your students become servant leaders?

October

"A few hundred years from now, it will not matter what my bank account was. The sort of house I lived in, or the kind of car I drove, but the world may be different because I was important in the life of a child."
~ Forest E. Witcraft

Daring to be Different

October 1st

"We must dare to be different, to point to ideals other than those of this world, testifying to the beauty of generosity, service, purity, perseverance, forgiveness, fidelity to our personal vocation,
prayer, the pursuit of justice and the common good,
love for the poor and social friendship."
- Pope Francis, "Christus Vivit: Post-Synodal Apostolic Exhortation", 2019

Daring to be different and living up to ideals that are not of this world have always been my calling. Generosity and service go hand in hand in my life. I have always enjoyed giving my expertise and materials and service to others, especially students and schools. I enjoy finding ways to provide my services at a reduced rate or at no cost.

I live with purity in the form of our special needs daughter, Ashley. She is pure in heart, mind, and body. Perseverance has always been a trait that I most admire. I will hire perseverance over great intellect or talent every time. I believe true success can only be found in perseverance.

Forgiveness is an ongoing process in my life. Every day I learn, every day I have an opportunity to forgive. I pray to be more forgiving. Social justice and the good for all, especially those in need, is the mission of our work. It has been the mission of my life.

- In conversation with a trusted friend, discuss the importance of perseverance in your life.

Forgiveness and Compassion

October 2nd

"For me, forgiveness and compassion are linked:
how do we hold people accountable for wrongdoing and
yet at the same time remain in touch with their humanity enough
to believe in their capacity to be transformed."
- bell hooks, *All About Love: New Visions*

In my better moments, I'm aware that those who have hurt me we're doing the best they could with what they knew at the time. There are infinite unknown concerns and stressors on all of us. I can never know someone else's motivations. They may not even know their own motivations. When we forgive, we let go of the expectations and dreams we had for the other person. Often when I feel hurt, it is because someone did not live up to being the person I thought they could be. Forgiveness requires that I allow them to be the person they are. When asked how he was able to forgive those that unjustly imprisoned him, Nelson Mandela said, "When I walked out of the gate, I knew that if I continued to hate those people, I was still in prison."

"Forgiveness is the only way to heal ourselves and to be free of the past. Without forgiveness, we remain tethered to the person who harmed us. We are bound in the chains of bitterness, tied together, trapped. Until we can forgive the person who harmed us, that person will hold the keys to our happiness; that person will be our jailor. When we forgive, we take back control of our own fate and our feelings. We become our own liberator."
- Archbishop Desmond Tutu and Mpho Tutu, *The Book of Forgiving: The Fourfold Path for Healing Ourselves and Our World*

- How do you see compassion connected to forgiveness?

The Gift

October 3rd

If you feel like there is work to be done, then be sure you are the one to do it. An idea comes to you because it finds you a willing and suitable host. If something comes into your vision, then there is something for you to do. Ask- "What would you have me do?" The answer will follow.

We are the gift that the world needs.

- What are you being called to do?

A Spider's Story

October 4th

There is an ancient story about a holy man and a spider. The holy man would come every day to the river and sit to pray. One day, while in prayer, he noticed a spider. The spider was on the farthest edge of a limb, which stretched out over the roaring river.

The holy man saw that the limb on which the spider was perched was cracked and about to break. Being aware that the spider would drown if the limb broke into the river, the holy man reached out his hand to the spider.

The spider stung him! The holy man gently cupped the spider in his hand and the spider stung him again! Finally placing the spider softly on the ground, the spider stung him again and asked, "Why did you save me? You knew it was my nature to sting."

The holy man replied, *"Just because it is your nature to sting, why should I deny my nature to save?"*

We are all both the holy man and the spider. It is our human nature to both save and sting. Do not deny either. That would be less than honest. When we sting, seek forgiveness. Our stinging comes from our need for survival. When we save, we claim our God-given inheritance. Spiders (ego-driven) sting and human beings (God-centered) save. Be the savior, no matter the consequence.

- With a trusted friend, discuss the two natures within each of us. The nature of the spider to sting, and the nature of the Holy Man to save.

Courageously Reconnecting Our Broken Pieces

October 5th

In this life, we have all been hurt and we have all hurt someone else. Life offers lesson after lesson. For the most part, we do not intend to hurt others and they don't intend to hurt us.

"Unintended hurt is as common as branches snapped by the wind."
- Mark Nepo, *The Book of Awakening: Having the Life You Want by Being Present to the Life You Have*

"Just as our only recourse to falling is getting up, our only recourse to hurting others is to acknowledge what we've done and clean up the mess. In 12 step groups and other support systems, this is called making amends."
- Mark Nepo, *The Book of Awakening: Having the Life You Want by Being Present to the Life You Have*

Making amends is an act of humility, forgiveness, and integrity. We own our behaviors and ask for forgiveness. Integrity restores trust. Trust connects us with our essential values. We learn by trusting that by sharing our diversity, we discover unity. In this life, we will feel both hurt and love. Our unity is formed when we overcome the hurt. Life is repaired and love is created when we courageously reconnect our broken pieces.

♦ In quiet reflection, are there people in your life that you need to make amends to? Draw on your courage and make amends.

Accessing Education's Greatest Human Resource

October 6th

In the political agenda, to reform education, we have forgotten a great time-proven truth: reform will not be achieved by standardized tests, teaching to the test, restructuring schools, privatizing schools, rewriting curriculum, or standardizing curriculum. We must not continue to oppress and repress teachers. The greatest human resource we have is our teachers. This has always been true, from Jesus and Socrates to Rosa Parks and Helen Keller. There are no role models without teachers. Teachers must be freed of political harassment. Teachers must be allowed to help lead, structure, and govern schools.

We must cherish the human heart.
We must educate the whole child.
We must return to our source, our teacher, for true reform.

- Who has been some of your best teachers?
- What life lessons have they taught you?

Misunderstandings

October 7th

Misunderstandings are less likely to occur when we assume a benevolent intention on everyone else's part and react accordingly.

Much of our stress and suffering comes from defining ourselves as lesser beings in contact with change, conflict, or someone else. Remember, our connection to the infinite is unbroken and undiminished. We can make mistakes without believing we are a mistake.

- What have you learned from some of your misunderstandings?

What is Essential?

October 8th

What is essential?

This is the question we must ask of all who are involved in education. Now is a crucial time. I am concerned that we are on the brink of losing a generation of students to testing and political agendas. It is long past time when we need to return management, decision-making, and leadership back to teachers and educators.

What is essential?

I believe the answers will impact our future.

♦ What is essential to you in education and the teaching and learning process?

If You Want…

October 9th

If you want a happy relationship…
bring happiness and positive energy to your relationship.

If you want cooperation…
be understanding and empathetic.

If you want freedom…
be responsible.

If you want trust…
be trustworthy.

- Be the change you want to see.

Be True to Who You Are

October 10th

When I make a commitment, I am in an intimate relationship with my soul. I am committed to my mission, to my sense of purpose in this life. This includes staying true to myself when things are difficult. This includes accepting my faults, mistakes, limitations, and aging. I am still learning to love myself, even when others do not. I am more concerned about being integrous with my soul than I am concerned with the approval of others. This is simultaneously difficult and essential. I embrace the Divinity that resides within me- the same Divinity that radiates in all life. I am bound to my truth.

- What is most true for you? Follow your truth.

Survival Through Cooperation

October 11th

There are many references to biology that justifies an animalistic struggle for life. We have been taught that nature is competitive and selfish. Survival of the fittest is part of many biology and philosophy curricula. Do you believe in survival of the fittest? Or is the truth of humanity found in survival of the kindest?

The reality in many minds and much of nature is survival through cooperation. The family of humanity has a long lineage of survival through cooperation. Empathy and connection are part of our DNA.

♦ How are you cooperating with your peers to create a school community?

The Road Less Taken

October 12th

"Two roads diverged in a wood, and I-I took the one less traveled by, and that has made all the difference."
- Robert Frost, "The Road Not Taken"

I look back on my choices. I have often chosen the less traveled road. I have followed the "still, small voice" that has called me to a deeper meaning and higher learning. Creativity, innovation, imagination, and a constant re-inventing of my life has led me to a unique wisdom. I follow the wisdom path traveled by Jesus, Buddha, Gandhi, Reverend Dr. Martin Luther King, Jr., and Mandela.

When I feel diminished or broken, I rest for a day or two and begin again. I read, pray, talk with my beloved wife Sandra, stay close to our daughter Ashley, and reconnect to my passion and mission.

We are all part of a divine spiritual birthright. We are eternal. We are ever evolving change agents of an ending we will not witness. The power to choose our path is a daily offering. Be your unique self, follow your passion. Travel the road less taken. It will make all the difference.

- What choices have you made in your life that brought you to a "less traveled" road?

Try

October 13th

Yoda says, “Do or do not, there is no try.”
I disagree.
I prefer the adage “try, try, try again”
My inner voice, my higher self
whispers, “try again”
Forgive
Forgive
Forgive
Even though there is nothing to forgive
All we do is try to love
Love, like God, comes in many distressing disguises
Love can be fear, hurt, anger or pain
At the source, everything is love
All we do is try to love
There is nothing to forgive
Try, try, try again
Love
Love
Love

- Reflect on the most recent time in your life when you made a repeated effort on a challenging task or problem.

Keep Dreaming

October 14th

When we are blessed with an idea or a dream that will serve the greater good, we must act on this calling. There have been times in my life that I have heard the "small, still voice" of spirit calling me to create something that will serve. I follow the voice, I gather resources, I plan, and I present the idea to those who have the ability to help make the dream a reality. Sometimes we meet with rejection, lack of support, or lack of understanding. This is simply life asking us- how important is this dream to you? Are we confident? Are we aligned with spirit in our creation? Rejection is not necessarily an accurate evaluation of the quality of your dream. Rejection very often is simply a statement of the mindset and heart of the critic.

I value feedback immensely. Remember, feedback is not evaluation. Feedback is specific, descriptive, observable, behavioral data about where you and I are together on a shared task. When we feel rejection, hold fast to your faith that is much greater than the opinions and fears of others.

If you believe in a dream, do not be put off by obstacles.

- What dream are you currently dreaming?

The Right Thing is: Kind, Respectful, and Empowering

October 15th

I truly believe that most human beings want to do the right thing. I believe the right thing is to be kind, respectful and empowering. We need to believe in each other's goodness. We need to practice acts of kindness and gratitude. Our wealth is in the spiritual. Our spiritual wealth is unlimited. It has no bounds.

The goodness of life, our spiritual wealth, belongs to everyone. The goodness of life is inclusionary. No one is left out. The better we give, the better we receive. We are all part of the whole. We are all connected to the infinite. Let our interactions be conscious of this Divine union. Let us practice unity consciousness until it is manifested in our daily lives.

- How are you working towards unity in your classroom and school?

Live Life on Purpose

October 16th

The most effective way to achieve our goals and dreams is to live our life on purpose. Specifically, fulfilling our sense of purpose in helping others to fulfill their sense of purpose. When we are all focused on our sense of purpose, stress will be reduced, and joy will be revealed.

"Our prime purpose in life is to help others."
- His Holiness the Dalai Lama

"Help others achieve their dreams,
and you will achieve your dreams."
- Les Brown

♦ How are you helping others achieve their dreams?

Dreams

October 17th

When we are no longer driven by the need for approval or fear of judgment…when the light of unconditional love in all humanity shines through our eyes…when we are on purpose…we will be aware, that, Providence opens all opportunities, even where we did not previously see any possibilities.

The universe listens and fulfills our dreams.

- In quiet reflection, focus on your dreams for your personal and professional life.

Speak Your Truth

October 18th

"It is by risking ourselves from one hour to another that we live at all."
- William James

Although I do not like conflict and throughout my life, I have often tried to avoid it, there is no way to avoid conflict. I am a passionate man, and I am very passionate in my mission to serve children in schools in Social Emotional Learning. I have found that when we are passionate in our mission, we will encounter conflict. When I have avoided conflict with others, I have created a deadly conflict in myself. When I have not shared my truth and passion, that same truth and passion festers inside me. When I speak my truth and address my mission, at some point I am in conflict with those who would like me to be someone else.

The cost for being authentic is someone will disapprove. There will be conflict with someone. The cost of not being real, the cost of being less than myself creates a series of little deaths inside of us. Trying to please everyone destroys our authenticity.

At 71 years old, I must speak my truth. Life is precious. Life is too short to appease everyone and suffer the little deaths that come with societal approval.

- In conversation with a trusted friend, discuss your experience with conflict. Focus on the moments you did not follow your truth or the times you did follow your truth.

The Secret to an Extraordinary Life

October 19th

Much of our anxiety and inner conflict comes from living in a world that drives us to perform for attention. The value is on what we do, what we accomplish, not on the essence of what matters.

We are encouraged and often applauded for our achievements. We are focused too much on getting attention, when the secret to a peaceful and fulfilling life is on giving attention.

Most recently our schools, teachers, and students are told they are only of value when they perform well on standardized tests. In our schools and work, we are conditioned to believe that to be a success, we must be special; score the highest, be the best, be number one. The reality of the secret to an extraordinary life is revealed when we devote ourselves to giving attention to others.

All of life comes alive with intrinsic value when we see and recognize that everything and everyone is special. The more we focus on getting attention rather than giving it, our unhappiness grows. It leaves us in a world of dissatisfaction and need. We are always dreaming of a future greatness. We always need someone else's approval. Our unity is in seeing the grace in all life.

When we see and give love, we touch the joy of spirituality. We are healthy and whole in celebrating all life. Give attention through service. Build your identity on finding beauty in all life. Find peace in celebrating life.

♦ How are you helping your students find their gifts and talents?

True Family

October 20th

"The bond that links your true family it's not one of blood,
but of respect and joy in each other's life.
- Richard Bach, *Illusions:*
The Adventures of a Reluctant Messiah

I've been working professionally with, for, and employing people for 50 years. My friend of 50 years, Joe, often says, "You don't hire people, you adopt them." When you are a part of my work team, on a variety of projects, you become a part of my family.

My goal was not to build a business. My goal was to build a process that help children, teachers, and schools be the best they could be. I want to help schools become Whole Child-Centered-emotionally safe, nurturing environments. Our work helps schools integrate social and emotional learning with academics. Our work is a catalyst for transformation.

Our core beliefs are respect for self and others, a sense of responsibility for everything you think, feel, say, and do, and developing healthy relationships. I am blessed to work with people I respect and love. They are all assets in my life. I feel tremendous joy as I watch and participate in the growth of my friends, colleagues, students, and schools.

- Who are the assets in your life?
- How are these people part of your spiritual journey?

The Highest Standards

October 21st

To commit our teaching as a loving service to our students transforms our work to a spiritual gift. The definition of excellence in education becomes a commitment to the highest standards of human development.

Are we kind?
Are we respectful?
Are we responsible?
Have we been kind to everyone with whom we interact?

All our actions become an opportunity to serve the greater good.

All our preparation, late night phone calls home, adapting lessons, and supporting the needs of the Whole Child become ingredients and contributions to World Service. Our smallest intervention serves the greater good, provides health and healing, and ennobles our profession.

- Rest in the knowledge that you have made a positive difference in the lives of students, parents, and colleagues.

Contribute to the Good

October 21st

"You cannot solve a problem by using the same kind of thinking we used when we created them."
- Albert Einstein

The challenges we are all currently facing will not be solved by sitting around a conference table discussing the problem. Each one of us is being called to act responsibly. We are all responsible for what we think, say, feel, and do. It is time to accept the call to heal ourselves, each other, and our planet. We can forgive and let go of any negative thoughts that impact our spirits. We can contribute to the good.

Know that there is a greater power of unconditional love at work in our life and in the lives of all humanity.

♦ What do you feel called to contribute to help our world heal? Sign up now!

Courage is Calling... Will We Answer the Call?

October 23rd

"From ancient times, a decline in courage
has been considered the first symptom of the end."
- Alexander Solzhenitsyn, Commencement Address at
Harvard University, "A World Split Apart", 1978

"If not you, who? If not now, when?"
- Hillel

Courage is always a risk. Like all the courageous people of history, we are at a pivotal moment.

Will we stand for character?
Will we speak the truth?
Will we conquer the fear of disapproval and follow our North Star?
Will we be people of character and values? Listen! Did you hear the call?

Our life's mission calls to us from deep inside our soul.
We each are invited to be all that we can be.

- What is calling to you?
- What commitment must you make?

Inspiration

October 24th

We are all human beings with infinite and endless possibilities. Inspiration is the beginning of moving forward and making our possibilities real. Inspiration moves us beyond our perceived limits.

When we are inspired, we are literally breathing in spirit. Inspiration, from the Latin "in spiritus", means to breathe in spirit. When we breathe in spirit, we are breathing in the Divine. We are breathing in God. When we breathe in spirit, everything is possible. We rise to the occasion. We embrace the dream. Our talents and abilities come to the surface.

Inspiration fills you with Divine energy.

- ♦ What inspires you?
- ♦ Who inspires you?
- ♦ How will you move forward with this inspiration?

I Rededicate Myself

October 25th

As I continue to study, reflect, and work to be a good, caring person, I do my best not to be judgmental. This continues to be a challenge. I am open and accepting, but I continue to struggle with past hurts. Particularly when someone has broken my trust. I find it very difficult to trust that person again.

I find there is a great wisdom in believing that every person is doing the best they can with what they know and what their life experience has been. When I allow myself to accept that truth, I can move to understanding. I can forgive and possibly be empathetic.

My life has been grounded in the core values of caring, compassion, trust, hard work, and integrity. I know what is right and wrong for *me.* I do not know what is right and wrong for *you.*

There is so much hate in our world now. We think we know what is right or wrong for everyone. We need to reclaim the beauty of perspective to see the world through the eyes and experience of the other. We need to work towards compromise or at least listen to each other.

I rededicate myself to acceptance and gratitude.

- Reflect on one person who you disagree with. Offer an opportunity for discussion and allow yourself to fully listen to their point of view.

Life is Constant Change

October 26th

Life is constant change. Motion is the lotion for our body's health. Motion is change and change is renewal.

We are renewed in body, mind, and spirit; and this renewal brings us deeper into the awareness of who we are.

We are wise to bring conscious thought into this change process. Let our thoughts be positive, uplifting, and generous.

Our relationships mirror back to us our core beliefs and values. Healthy relationships are mutually supportive, nurturing, loving, and beneficial. We allow ourselves to be vulnerable and trusting and come to a deeper connection. We thrive on this connection.

We are all one in spirit. We love and accept ourselves and our healthy relationships.

- What change is happening in your life at this time?
- How can you embrace this change process?
- What good can you see coming from your acceptance of this change?

Affirmation of Humanity

October 27th

Miriam Elkes, a survivor of the Holocaust, often told her son that throughout her ordeal, she always carried two things on her person: a piece of bread, and a piece of comb. She kept the bread in case someone needed it more than her. Each night she would comb her hair to affirm that she was still a human being.

What do you and I have within us, or on us that can help others in their time of need? What do we do daily to affirm our humanity? No matter how challenged we are, there is always something we can give to another in the world. The greater our challenge, the more essential it is to do something each day that affirms our humanity.

- What do you do on a daily basis to affirm your humanity?

Maturity

October 28th

Something eternal has been born in me. I have no choice but to nurture it until it reaches its full growth and maturity.

I have been studying, experiencing, practicing, and teaching to become my best self for the past 71 years. I am aware that we all have been blessed with the sacred spark of Divinity within each of us. I know that spark grows and blossoms as we serve others.

I continue to feel deeply called to a life of service. I am gravely concerned for our nation, our families, our communities, and our children, *all our children*. I have no interest in a political debate. Either I am serving the greater good, or I am not. It is that simple. The greater good is quite simple to me.

Am I kind?
Am I respectful?
Am I compassionate?
Am I responsible?
Am I conscious and aware?
Do I seek to be a better person today than I was yesterday?
Will I make a greater contribution to our world today than I did yesterday?

♦ How are you a better person today than you were yesterday?

We are One Sacred Family

October 29th

"Fear, pain, and worry make us retreat,
while great love, and great suffering break down those barriers."
- Mark Nepo

Will we be a society, a culture, a people that lives in fear and pushes people away because we perceive them as different? Can we be a society, a culture, a people that lives in great love and compassion and invites those we see as different to come close and teach us?

Will we be self-serving, in need of control and untrustworthy or can we be kind, generous, servant leaders who are trusting?

Fear tricks us into believing that retreating, protecting, and excluding will keep us safe. Love welcomes and reminds us that we are one within our diversity. We are essentially more alike than we are different.

"We are born whole but need each other to be complete."
- Plato

We are here to connect. We are here to be a unique part of an infinite whole. It is essential to tell our story. It is equally essential to listen to the stories of others. When we share the vulnerability of our stories, we find that we are not alone. Every human life is sacred. We are one sacred family.

- How did you make a connection today?
- How did you share your story and listen to the story of others?

What Could Have Broken Me, Made Me Who I Am

October 30th

A spirit deep inside me has always invited me to do more, bounce back, and keep going. I have come to know that spirit as my unconditionally loving God. Our special needs daughter, Ashley, has faced countless health and life crisis. In each challenge, I found myself going deeper into prayer. Even though frightened, I found myself meeting each new challenge head on. I'm not good at avoiding. I am not good at compartmentalizing. In my life, everything is connected, everything is personal. And in every crisis my family has faced with Ashley, I found myself looking for the ring of light. Where is the hope? Where is the lesson? How can I be better? Because Ashley is so physically challenged, my own internal challenges are revealed to me. I look at my own imperfections and I share my pain and vulnerability without shame.

Throughout Ashley's 39 years, Sandra and I have looked for doctors, therapists, and answers to help her heal. I now know that she is not here to be healed. She is the healer. Ashley cannot speak, cannot make a conscious movement, she is tube fed and diapered. She has healed my life by her presence, her unconditionally loving presence. I have learned that presence, Ashley's presence, is deep spiritual listening. She is totally open and vulnerable; she has no defense. She is beyond cognition. I've needed to let go of old mindsets, of what is normal. We live beyond normal. We live, with Ashley in the mystical. We live in grace. We live in love.

- What experiences have you have that did not fit with society's definition of normal?
- How have these experiences enhanced your life?

Peace of Mind

October 31st

"It is not easy to find happiness in ourselves,
and it is not possible to find it elsewhere."
- Agnes Repplier

Throughout the course of my life, the biggest roadblocks to happiness and peace of mind have been the concerns of others, the concerns of the world and myself. My training and belief confirm that I have been my biggest roadblock, by far, to my peace of mind.

As I've grown in authenticity and vulnerability, I find that I get lost in feeling sorry for myself and I also get lost in judgment of myself and others.

Even though I've been lost at times, I still have found the true path repeatedly. The essence of the Divine in each of us always beckons us forward to truth and lights our way.

- With a trusted friend, share one of your core values that acts as your north star, and keeps you moving forward in challenging times.

Gratitude

November and December

Our last two months of the year will be spent in reflection on the powerful and essential skill of gratitude.

Two of my most favorite words to share with another human being are "thank you." I love to show appreciation and kindness. Gratitude invites us to pause and reflect on all the people, places, and things that enhance our lives. When we express our gratitude, we affirm all the good in our lives. We acknowledge other people and that builds and strengthens our relationships and health.

November

"Gratitude turns what we have into enough."
~ Aesop

A Prayer for Humanity

November 1st

Dear God,

I continue to feel your unconditional love permeating my heart and mind. I see your love and acceptance in every diverse face. We are all loved, no exceptions.

In this unconditionally loving universe, everyone is welcomed. Everyone is accepted. Everyone is valued. Everyone is loved. No one is excluded.

May we all share this love with open hearts and minds.

May we all be together in loving humanity.

- Share an act of gratitude with someone who you feel you might have excluded in the past.

Possibilities

November 2nd

Many of us are fortunate to know that we are blessed to feel appreciation and gratitude for the simple pleasures of life…to feel the wonder of a flower in bloom…to feel the awe of a crimson and pink sunset…to feel the ecstasy of holding the hand of someone you have loved for over 45 years.

I am so grateful to wake up and think of possibilities. Each morning, I let go of the past and think of the wonderful, infinite possibilities that are waiting for me. I focus on my dreams and my goals.

I live my life with gratitude and appreciation. I live in a comfortable home. I have a warm shower. I have a warm bed to sleep in and a variety of foods to nourish me. I can calm my mind, release my stress, and open myself to new possibilities.

- Make a list of all the things you have that you are grateful for.

There Are No Small Actions

November 3rd

I don't remember consciously inviting this difficult time period into my life. I pray to move through this as soon as possible. I am aware that in the past, difficult times have been good for my soul and strengthened my character.

Difficult times have invited me to gather my character traits, virtues, faith, and love to face adversity.

"If you bring forth what is within you,
what is within you will save you."
- Adapted from the Gospel of Thomas

Difficult times liberate us from ego-driven- me, me, me. Today's questions appear difficult. I search deeper and longer for truth. I join with my unseen allies, spirit, angels, and unconditional love. I listen to the "still, small voice". The universe speaks to me, and I am engaged in a relationship with the whole world. We all thrive on *inter*dependence. We are all *inter*connected. This is our opportunity. Pour your love and purpose into every day. Be yourself. Be fully authentic. There are no small actions. The world needs you. Now!

- With a trusted fiend discuss the connections in your life that you are grateful for.

Share Your Love and Gratitude

November 4th

"Too often, we underestimate the power of a touch, a smile, a kind word, a listening ear, an honest compliment, or the smallest act of caring, all of which have the potential to turn a life around."
- Dr. Leo Buscaglia

I have had the privilege to spend many hours with those in their final days. Universally, we want to know; did our life have meaning? Did it matter that we were here? We all want to feel that our lives had meaning and purpose. We all have contributed something special to this world. We all leave something meaningful.

Do not wait until someone is leaving this life; let them know now. Tell people you love and appreciate them. Let them know they have contributed to your life. Let them know they have made a positive impact, a difference in life.

When we acknowledge and affirm each other, we transform our lives.

Be generous and abundant with your compliments.

Extend loving kindness to everyone.

♦ Reach out to a beloved friend or family member and let them know how grateful you are for them.

Sandra

November 5th

My wife, Sandra is full of love and joy. Most mornings you can find her singing a happy tune. Sandra has an inner light that never ceases to shine, even when we are challenged.

Sandra is devoted to her family and is a good and loving friend. She has given the past 39 years of her life to our special needs daughter, Ashley. In her 24/7 service, she finds a deep satisfaction. She knows she is fulfilling her purpose. Sandra has a deep and loving faith. Her life is not easy.

An average day is up at 7:00 AM, then starts Ashley's medications, breathing treatments, percussion treatments, and diapering. Tube feeding also begins at the same time. On most days, Ashley is up in her wheelchair by 10:30 AM; and Sandra begins other tasks. At noon, it is medicine time again, at 5:00 PM, it is feeding time and medicine time again at 7:00 PM. At 10:00 PM, Ashley is put into bed and the breathing treatment, percussion treatment, and diapering begin again. Through all this exhausting work, Sandra has serenity. She is resolved in her loving care. She finds great joy in giving herself for the good of others.

♦ Express your gratitude to someone who has devoted their life to others.

Empathy

November 6th

Empathy does not make us soft. Empathy makes us fully human. When we can understand those who feel very differently than we do, they become more human in our eyes.

It is very easy to be judgmental. It takes great effort and empathy to seek to know and understand. We can never know the history and challenges of those whose wounds we do not understand. We have all been broken. We all will fall, and fail, again and again. Empathy says, "Judge not lest ye be judged."

- With a trusted friend, share your gratitude for what you have experienced and shared together.

Act for the Good of Humanity

November 7th

Let us keep ourselves honest, truthful, caring, and kind. Let us practice gratitude, fairness, compassion, and empathy.

Let us strive to be the person that God made us to be. Respect all life and care for each other.

Life is short.

Be a person of good character.

Act for the good of humanity.

♦ What is one small action you can take today for the good of humanity?

Compassion and Caring

November 8th

When we focus on love, compassion, empathy, and integrity those values move from us to impact and uplift others beyond our physical sphere of influence.

Compassion and caring for our fellow humans connect us and promote understanding and unity. We discover the Divine in each of us.

When we see others through eyes of compassion, we see the best in our fellow human beings.

- Who needs you to see them with compassionate eyes?
- Seek them out and share your caring and compassion.

Dream Your Unique Dream

November 9th

"Do not be conformed to this world,
but be transformed by the renewal of your mind."
- Romans 12:2, *The Holy Bible, English Standard Version*

When you have an idea or dream, don't look for approval from a social group. We surrender our authenticity and leadership when we seek approval from a social group.

Leaders step forward and serve the greater good. They look upward and onward. They dream a vision beyond the social conformity.

Move ahead with courage.

Dream your unique dream.

- What unique dream do you still need to share with the world?
- Be grateful this dream was sent to you.

Appreciate

November 10th

Let us appreciate the moments we have together. So many of us have faced challenge, trauma, pain, and grief these last 3 years. For me, it was heart surgery two years ago.

I find happiness when I can appreciate those in my life just the way they are. When I can see the unique beauty in each person in my life, I am filled with love. When there is love within us, then love grows into the world.

There is no need to fix or change, just appreciate. We have so few moments together.

Let us appreciate and love.

Let us see the sacred in all life.

- Send an act of love and appreciation to someone who is important to you.

Living in Understanding, Empathy, and Compassion is Our Next Evolution

November 11th

I care deeply about humanity. We must come to the place of understanding that we are all a part of a beautifully diverse global community.

Our human history is abundant with examples of hatred, neglect, racism, slavery, and war. Pursuing only our narcissistic interests will end in suffering and death.

Our best hope for the future is education. Not only the old, reading writing, and arithmetic, but a new education of the heart. We need social, emotional, and ethical teaching and learning. We need to teach conversation, community building, and cooperation.

Empathy is in our DNA. We are all one global family. We must respect and learn our differences and rejoice and celebrate our similarities.

We all need acceptance and love.

- How can you show acceptance and gratitude for your students and colleagues?

Laughter is the Effervescence of Life

November 12th

I greatly appreciate those individuals who sit lightly in our world. I love when we can laugh at ourselves. My nature is a bit on the serious side. I am naturally introspective and thoughtful; I enjoy deep conversations.

I also love laughter. I find it healing and refreshing. I think a good sense of humor; especially self-effacing humor, is essential for a healthy life. I greatly appreciate people who can laugh at themselves.

I love when our lives bubble up with joy and laughter. Divinity is playful, full of joy, and has a wonderful sense of humor.

I am grateful for laughter and play.

♦ Share your gratitude for those who help you laugh and feel joy.

Shine the Light of Love

November 13th

No harm can do lasting damage when you know God is unconditional and is with you.

When we enter a painful period in our lives, we do not need to stay in the darkness. While in the darkness, feel all there is to feel. Feel the pain, feel the fear. Feel all that you feel fully. Then turn on the light. Go to your sources of love and light. What are your sources of love and light?

For me they are my faith. My faith is an unconditional loving God. I do believe I am held in the palm of unconditional love. Another source of love and light is my wife, Sandra. She is limitless kindness, compassion, deep caring, and love. There is also our angelic daughter Ashley. Although unable to speak or consciously move, Ashley emanates divine love constantly.

My morning prayer and meditation are tools that turn on the light. Yoga, nature, water, and sun also bring me the warmth of love.

I choose to shine the light of love on every situation in my life.

- What are the everyday experiences you are grateful for?
- Journal about this gratitude or share with a trusted friend.

Our Healthy Relationships

November 14th

Empathy and compassion are created through relationships and a commitment to something or someone greater than you.

Our relationships vary in degree and intensity and are based on trust, honesty, integrity, and caring. We create authentic relationships based on our self-awareness and social awareness.

All healthy relationships begin with connection. When we nurture our connection, we seek to honor, empower, and uplift the spirit in each other. We bring our authenticity, vulnerability, and integrity to our friends, family, and workmates. We bring as much or more than we receive.

Let us all base our relationships on authenticity, empathy, compassion, and generosity.

- List all the relationships you are grateful for and the lessons you have learned from these relationships.

Authentic and Transparent

November 15th

Be at peace. Practice being authentic and transparent.

Spirit is within each of us. When we are at peace with our authentic self, we replace fear with love. In this love, we find self-acceptance and share our best self with the world.

As we give, we receive.

When we are authentic and transparent, we form relationships that recognize and honor our authenticity and transparency.

We are at peace.

- Journal about your moments of authenticity and transparency.
- Give thanks for being your true self.

Forgiveness

November 16th

I am aware that I am holding myself captive when I fail to forgive. I have known for many years that forgiveness initially benefits the forgiver.

I must continue to work on my willingness to forgive. When I hold onto some past hurt or perceived injustice, my loving heart is blocked. My essential nature, like yours, is Divine love. Forgiveness is part of that Divine nature.

I do not feel any satisfaction in revisiting the old hurt and pain. Perhaps, it is just comfortable and familiar. I know that when I shut down one loving pathway of my heart, I also shut down the greater love in my heart. We cannot selectively shut out parts of our love.

I know now, my job is to hold nothing back. When we forgive, we feel joy and the power of love.

- What or who calls for your forgiveness?

Can You Hear That?

November 17th

"All over the sky a sacred voice is calling your name."
- Black Elk

You are compassion, empathy, truth, trust, and love. Deep, abiding love. Unconditional love.

Can you hear that?
Can you accept that?
Can you own that?
You are an emanation of Divinity.

No matter how many lies you and the world have told you about yourself, you are not anything other than love.

You are part of the unconditional loving energy that creates the universe.

- Reflect on the acts of love you have offered today.

One Human Family

November 18th

The essential concern for humanity is a lack of understanding and love. The answer to reconnecting is the ability to see everyone as a member of our human family. We are all more similar than we are different.

When we encounter someone we perceive is different, it would be wise to ask ourselves…

How would I connect with this person if they were a family member whom I loved?

♦ Reach out to someone you perceive to be different than yourself. Invite them for a discussion about family. Be aware of what you learn and how you feel as the discussion unfolds.

Hero's Journey

November 19th

"We have not even to risk the adventure alone
for the heroes of all time have gone before us."
- Joseph Campbell, *The Power of Myth*

We are all on a hero's journey through this life. We confront great challenges: heart surgery, pandemic, social justice, trauma. In each of our hero's journey, we face times of transition and transformation. If we are awake and aware, each step of the journey reveals hidden truths and talents. We find the great treasure of ourselves. We find authenticity, transparency, vulnerability, and courage.

Life calls us to adventure. Through birth, death, and rebirth, we find the great expression of life. Our life! We create our greatest work of art. If we refuse the call to life, we stagnant and die long before our physical death. If we accept the call and show up each day with open hearts and minds, we are rewarded with new life and new adventure. Through each adventure, we return newly empowered and with greater wisdom. Like the characters in Oz, we find greater courage, wisdom, and love. Our lives are enriched, and we return to life and life is enhanced for all.

◆ What current adventure are you going through at this time in your life?

Every Contribution Made in Love Counts Forever

November 20th

I believe that in our lives there are moments of awareness and awakening. Something, often miraculous, occurs to remind us that our life is not a fluke. We are here on purpose. In these moments, I believe our soul is calling out to us.

Wake up! This is not a dress rehearsal. It is time to straighten up and fly right.

These soulful moments invite us to heal our relationships with ourselves and others. They invite us to find peace in our hearts and in our actions. We are invited to act for the greater good of humankind and our precious earth.

The soul knows we are all part of a cosmic unity. We are all co-creating emanations of God's unconditional love.

Welcome everyone. We are being called together to awaken to the essential work of life.

Love.

- In quiet reflection, meditate on all the love you have been given today.

Journey of Self-Discovery

November 21st

"Every person, all the events of your life
are there because you have drawn them there,
what you choose to do with them is up to you."
- Richard Bach, *Illusions: The Adventures of a Reluctant Messiah*

Everything that happens in our lives presents us with opportunities for significant learning.

We evolve, and the truth of who we truly are is revealed.

There are no judgments or punishments, only lessons.

It is our birthright to learn and grow.

There are no accidents.

Everything is occurring for our growth and development.

We are wise to ask; "What am I learning from this experience?"

We are grateful to be on this journey of self-discovery.

- What are you currently learning?
- How are you currently giving?

I Feel the Challenges of Our World

November 22nd

I feel the challenges of our world. There is great complexity. None of us alone can solve the challenges of our complex world.

We need to know that the choices we make contribute to the resolution of social and global concerns. We are responsible for each other and our planet. We cannot leave it for someone else to solve. The time is now.

How do I care for the health and safety of those without a home?
How do I intervene with race and ethnic hatred and violence?
How do I provide enough food for starving children?
How do I stand for peace in a time of war?

The answer lives in me, in my spirit, in my soul. To change the world, I must change myself. To change myself, I must change my heart. I must risk being an example of love and acceptance. I must forgive. I must work for unity. I must speak for peace and harmony.

Love is the only sane and satisfactory response to the challenges of the world.

- What one action can you take today to help someone else?

Let Us Remember

November 23rd

Let us remember this is not the first time our nation has felt divided. On March 4th, 1861, five weeks before the Civil War began, newly elected President Abraham Lincoln opened his heart and spoke these words:

"We are not enemies, but friends. We must not be enemies. Though passion may have strained, it must not break our bonds of affection. The mystic chords of memory, stretching from every battlefield and patriot grave to every living heart and hearthstone all over this broad land, will yet swell the chorus of the Union who again touched, as surely will be by the better angels of our nature."

- Abraham Lincoln, "First Inaugural Address"

♦ Reach out to someone you perceive as different and offer your friendship.

We Need Each Other

November 24th

We marvel at the sun, moon, and stars. We love the mountains, oceans, beaches, and deserts. Do we not see the beauty of the humans that pass by us every day?

Every person we see is a unique and marvelous aspect of creation.

Today, we see so much division and separation. We need to see the Divine in our fellow humans. We need to treat each other with empathy, compassion, and love.

When we are born, we all must have human contact, or we die. We thrive on human connection. We are all part of the same life force.

"No man is an island entire of itself,
every man is a piece of the continent, a part of the main."
- John Donne, *Devotions upon Emergent Occasions*

We need each other.

♦ Contact someone who you haven't spoken to in a long while. Ask to visit together and share your life experiences.

Living With Integrity

November 25th

As a young man there were times when I was crippled with loneliness. The need to be liked made me overly sensitive to the negativity and perceived rejection by those whom I felt in need of their acceptance.

In my maturity, I have come to love and appreciate my alone time. I no longer seek or need the approval of those who do not really know me. I'm living my vocation with integrity.

I've experienced significant generosity in my 50 years of teaching. I reflect on the hospitality of educators in Athens, Illinois. I was there for professional development programing on Student Assistance Programs, and I was informed that one of the members of the staff was preparing lunch for me.

Unbeknownst to me, I was transported with a few other staff to her home. A very modest house, you might even say in a bit of disrepair. From this seemingly poor environment, I was honored with an elaborate Thanksgiving meal.

I was made welcome. I was an honored guest. There were no politics, no defense, no offense. I was invited to be part of their family.

"My house is your house, my joy is your joy,
my sadness is your sadness, and my life is your life."
- Henry Nouwen

◆ Give thanks for all the blessings in your life.

What Can We Do?

November 26th

"Even the strongest hands can lose their grip, the greatest minds can become cloudy, the biggest hearts can break.
So be kind. Just always be kind."
- Anonymous

We must teach each other and our children to have "good hearts". We must cultivate respect and trust for each other. We must be concerned for the rights, feelings, and general well-being of everyone.

Education is primarily serving others and leaving the world a little bit better than how we found it. We can all give time, connection, attention, laughter, hope, and love.

- Who needs your precious time now?

We Need Other People

November 27th

We need to connect to other people to be fully human. We need other people to trust, to laugh with, to treat with kindness and love.

When I am challenged by the people, I perceive to be difficult, I find that when I reflect and pray, I find answers.

In these challenging and difficult moments, I can decide who I really am and who I want to be.

If we want a country that is more understanding, then I need to be more understanding. If we want a country that is more accepting, then I need to be more accepting. If we want a country that is more loving, then I need to be more loving. We change the world with one caring choice at a time.

"…love thy neighbor as thyself."
- Matthew 12:31, *The Holy Bible, King James Version*

- What is one thing you can do for your neighbor?

"My Life is My Message"

November 28th

The lives we are living are a clear demonstration of what we believe. Our lives communicate to the world all that we think, feel, and believe.

Take time to reflect on the things you say and do, on the company you keep, and the messages you send. How are our lives contributing to the greater good?

Let us give ourselves in love and sacrifice to our fellow humans. Be generous with your spirit and your actions. A kind word, a caring action, a friendly smile, and hello can bring light into the world.

- Who needs you now?

Begin Now!

November 29th

"And so, we lift our gazes, not to what stands between us,
but what stands before us."
- Amanda Gorman, Inaugural Poem,
"The Hill We Climb", 2021

The work of coming together and healing our separation begins in the heart and soul of each one of us. If healing is to happen, and I believe it will, it will be made real by each one of us. No one will do it for us. The answer to healing our national divide can be found in the infinite potential and possibility of our Divine heritage.

We have joined together after hurricanes, tornadoes, floods, tsunamis, war, and terror attacks. Let us join together for all those who go to bed hungry. For all those who fear for their lives. For all those who have been abused and degraded. For all those who have experienced hatred, racism, sexism, and trauma.

Each one of us is called to heal our world.

Begin now!

♦ What act of healing can you offer now?

The Higher the Walls

November 30th

The higher the walls we build, the more we are imprisoned by fear. If we invest our energy in feeling safe and secure from those we perceive as different, we will paradoxically feel less secure.

Physical walls and psychological walls which are created to keep the "others" out, also keep us imprisoned in our limited perspective.

"I believe appreciation is a holy thing- that when we look for what's best in a person we happen to be with at the moment, we're doing what God does all the time. So, in loving and appreciating our neighbor, we are participating in something sacred."

- Fred Rogers, *The World According to Mister Rogers: Important Things to Remember*

♦ In quiet reflection, think of one wall that needs to come down in your world.

December

"When gratitude becomes an essential foundation in our lives, miracles start to appear everywhere."
~ Emmanuel Dalgher

Faith and Diversity

December 1st

All life and human growth, at some point, asks us to adapt to what is unfamiliar to us. Faith in ourselves and our ability to meet new people and situations is essential for our health, well-being, and growth. Most of us feel safe and secure in our homes. Many of us are comfortable in our community. When we are in unfamiliar surroundings, we get frightened and feel defensive.

Our faith invites us to adapt and learn when the environment, culture, language, skin color, or food is different.

Our faith is essential in building bridges and closing cultural gaps.

Our faith gives us an opportunity to grow.

Faith is the key to opening our minds and hearts so that we can love each other.

♦ In conversation with a trusted friend, discuss the aspects of your faith and how your beliefs can bring you closer to others.

One Spiritual Family

December 2nd

"One God and Father of all, who is above all,
and through all, and in you all."
- Ephesians 4:6, *The Holy Bible, New King James Version*

Love and faith respect *all* people.

Our spiritual family includes every ethnicity, religion, language, and culture.

I pray for the love and faith to respect and be kind to all people.

I communicate acceptance and empathy to all who are different than me.

I am grateful that we are all one in the same spiritual family.

◆ Today consciously smile or wave and say hello to a passing stranger.

Love Lives Forever

December 3rd

True friendship is everlasting because true love lives forever. In loving friendships, our hearts speak to each other.

Love continues beyond our physical death. When we love deeply that love ripples out into the world and touches many other lives.

- In quiet reflection, consciously send ripples of love into the world.

You Are Sacred

December 4th

The stress, tension, anxiety, and fear that we experience is the baggage of our life. Every day, make time to quiet your mind, go within and feel the flow of Divinity.

When you speak and act, remember to the best of your ability, to be understanding. Practice non-attachment. Let go of your need to control and someone else's need to control.

Cultivate your gifts.

Share your joy.

Be kind.

Just be kind.

- Share one simple act of kindness today.

You Belong

December 5th

"You are a child of the universe, no less than the trees and the stars; you have a right to be here."
- Max Ehrmann, "Desiderata"

You all have a right to be here. You are an essential part of the universe. Life would be lost without you. When you feel a sense of separation and isolation, remember you are part of one unconditionally loving life.

You belong in this life because you are here now. You belong to our universal family. We are one love living together. You are part of creation. The moon, the sun, and the stars are our family.

You belong.

- Look up at the stars on a clear night. Be aware of your place in the universe.
- Offer a thought or prayer of gratitude.

What We Put Our Attention on Grows

December 6th

Sometimes I need to stop, think, reflect, and remember how blessed my life is. I'm living, I am breathing, and I am still able to make choices.

Life has taught me that complaining about our lot in life gets us nowhere. I don't like complaining to myself or others. We all have challenges, both internal and external. We all must do the work required to meet our personal challenges. We all have difficult periods in our lives, and we all have melancholy days.

I find we must always spend more of our time remembering and practicing what works. Affirm and acknowledge those around us who speak and stand up for the good and positive in life. What we put our attention on grows. We must choose to focus on supporting all life, in all its evolutions. This brings us to greater truth and greater trust in the universe.

- ♦ In reflection, focus on one character trait you would like to ignite or grow.
- ♦ Create an action plan for the growth of that character trait and share the plan with a trusted friend.

For the Wellness of Humanity

December 7th

"I'm convinced of this:
good done anywhere is good done everywhere...
as long as you're breathing,
it's never too late to do some good."
- Maya Angelou

My grandfather used to say, "As long as you're breathing, there is work to do." I thought he meant the work we needed to do on the farm. Now I know he was talking about a much greater responsibility. We need deep, empathetic listening and compassionate, courageous action to serve the needs of our human family. We can no longer turn away from unconscious bias and the impact of our choices. We are all responsible for taking the actions that are needed to awaken and serve the greater good.

Love and service are at the heart of our efforts to connect. We are one interconnected whole. When anyone hurts, we all hurt. When anyone is diminished, we are all diminished. This is empathy. This is our birthright and responsibility. We can all thrive. We all are emanations of one unified whole.

Let us compassionately and courageously act for the wellness of all humanity.

◆ Do one thing today that will benefit the well-being of your community.

Love…

December 8th

Love is a way of being in the world.

It is more than something we give and/or get.

Love transforms the world.

We become grateful and we recognize grace.

Love is more than an emotion.

Love is more than an attitude and more than what we do.

Love is who we are.

- Who in your life needs your love?

Happy Birthday Sandra

December 9th

December 9th is my beautiful wife's 74th birthday. Sandra and I have been married for 45 years and she is quite simply the finest human being I've ever met in my life. Sandra is my role model and inspiration. Sandra is the kind of person songs and poems are written about. Her dedication and commitment to our special needs daughter has kept her alive and well for 39 years. Wherever I am, I speak about Sandra and Ashley. Sandra is commitment, she is empathy, she is compassion, she is faith she is unconditional love.

As I write this, Sandra is comforting Ashley in intensive care. She has not left her bedside since we entered the hospital. Ashley has pneumonia, she is intubated and on a ventilator. I marvel at her strength and positivity. Sandra makes friends with every caregiver in intensive care. No one gets away without being fully human. Sandra will love you until your walls melt. Her boundless energy brings bright light to everyone in the hospital.

Ashley continues to improve, and Sandra continues to shine her light on Ashley, our family, and everyone in her world. Sandra reminds me every day, that the greatest among us are not the brilliant, not the most innovative, or the wealthiest or most creative. The brightest lights in humanity are the kindest. Sandra shines her light through a beacon of kindness.

- Share your kindness with freedom and abundance.

Success

December 10th

"Success is not measured by the heights one attains,
but by the obstacles one overcomes in its attainment."
- Booker T. Washington

Those of us who have experienced success know we are not better than anyone else. The truly successful do not act with arrogance or dominance. Those who have been successful know that along with their hard work, they are blessed. The truly successful become stewards for the success of others. We help others grow and blossom into their greatness. We share responsibility to enhance the greatness of everyone.

"When you are inspired by some great purpose, some extraordinary project, all your thoughts break their bonds. Your mind transcends limitation, your consciousness expands in every direction, and you find yourself in a great, new, and wonderful world. Dormant forces, faculties and talents become alive, and you discover yourself to be a greater person by far than you ever dreamed yourself to be."
- Patanjali

- Who needs your help today?
- Reach out and offer your assistance.
- Do something to benefit another human being.

Ashley's Love

December 11th

Ashley's love is everywhere. It is in the sun that warms me and the rain that brings me solitude. Her love is in the gentle deer and scampering squirrel. Her love speaks to me when I am alone in our home and startles me when the whole family is home as if to say, "Don't leave me out of the conversation."

She is in my dreams and my prayers and meditation. She is in my mind, my heart, and my soul. In a unique and profound way, I am almost happy.

She walks with me, and she talks with me. Our relationship and our love continue. I can hear her say, "How silly Daddy, don't you know unconditional love can never die?"

Ashley was and is unconditional love. I am so grateful for the blessing that is Ashley.

♦ In quiet reflection, think of a beloved friend or family member who has passed from this earthly life and have a conversation with them in your mind and heart.

Work and Home

December 12th

I have always loved this Work.
I have always loved you, listener, student, friend.
I have always loved my friends.

I have always loved this Work.
I have always loved you, listener, student, friend.
I have always loved my family.

Somedays I am barely able to stand.
Most days I am thrilled to be able to walk.

I am still sharing the message.
I am still answering the call.
I am here with you, my voice, my heart, my soul.

After 50 years on the road, I am still here.
The road is long, dark, cold, ice and snow- hours away from home.
I have never forgotten where I've been.
I am clear on where I am going.
Every speech, every class, every conversation is a step homeward.

My friends are always in my heart.
My daughter has always been my angelic guide.
My sons continue to be my teachers.
Sandra is my love.

I always find my way Home.

- What is your Work? How do you find your way Home?

Miracles

December 13th

The fact that you are alive and reading- this is a miracle. Miracles are not only about people who walk on water or fly through the air. Miracles are people like you who wake up, even though you know the day will be challenging, and you still choose to get out of bed.

We have survived so much, a pandemic, life threatening surgeries, the loss of loved ones and the fear of our own breaking.

Your life has a special purpose. You are here on purpose. You are a breathing, walking, talking miracle. Whomever you are, old, young, strong, weak, rich, poor- you are alive. You are a miracle.

- Share your miraculous self with others today. Share your love.

I Have Been Feeling...

December 14th

I have been feeling "How is it that I am here, and Ashley is not?" I see her everywhere. In my office, in the spot where her wheelchair sat, in her bedroom where we prayed together and still do. She is here and yet not. Her soft, deep, brown eyes. Her baby-smelling hair. Her little, tiny fingers. Her perfect little nose.

The sun still comes up in the morning. The moon still moves through its cycles. We still get mail. Traffic is still busy. Everyone is rushing somewhere, and I wonder where do I want to go? I am disoriented. I am confused. She is here, but not here. I want to scream at disinterested people passing by. "Don't you know my precious angel is gone?" "Do you know how it feels to have unconditional love taken from you?"

So, I stumble in my new life, knowing she is in her new life, blessing and loving me as she always has, and always will.

I know unconditional love can never be taken from you. It just moves through you in a different form.

- Where do you go when you feel disconnected? Share your thoughts and feelings with a trusted friend.

Road of Healing

December 15th

"If suffering alone taught, all the world would be wise, since everyone suffers. To suffering must be added mourning, understanding, patience, love, openness, and the willingness to remain vulnerable."
- Anne Morrow Lindbergh, *Gift from the Sea*

This has been my journey these past few months. I pray to stay open and vulnerable to life's experiences. I hope that with time and love, I continue to move forward, not move on, but move forward. Move forward into greater strength, less fear, and greater health and wholeness. This being healthy is hard work, 24/7, diligent, disciplined, committed work.

As I travel this road of healing, I take my time, I pause, I notice, and I find gratitude.

I sense others who may need my help and I stay open to the help of others.

- With a trusted friend, discuss where you are on the road of healing. Ask for the help you need. Ask for what help you can give.

Hope

December 16th

Hope is such a powerful and beautiful concept. Where there is hope, there is light. Hope is the flickering candle in the darkest night. Hope is spirit shining deeply within us.

Hope is our loved ones whispering, "All is good." I am happy, I am full of peace.

Hope reminds us that death is not the end of life. Death is a passageway to new life.

Hope is the essence of life itself bubbling up, effervescent, flowering in the spring snow.

I hear my daughter in the bird song of early spring. I see her in the fawn that stops to nibble the new growth on the side of the trail. I feel her in the breeze that she so loved.

Her love and presence continue.

- What is your greatest hope?
- With a trusted friend, share your hopes and dreams.

Love and Approve of Yourself

December 17th

"Remember, you have been criticizing yourself for years and it hasn't worked. Try approving of yourself and see what happens."
- Louise Hay, *You Can Heal Your Life*

We are emanations of Divine love. See the light and love that is in your fellow humans. We are here to offer all the good that is within us.

We must be open to the joy, peace, and love that is our birthright. Be aware of your true nature and shower the world with your abundant gifts.

We are each here to shine God's loving light upon the earth.

Love and approve of yourself.

Shine your light and be aware and appreciate the light in others.

- ♦ Make a list of all the qualities you like about yourself. If you have difficulty, ask a trusted friend for help.

I Am All That You Taught Me to Be

December 18th

When I peek into your bedroom, I can feel your presence. Your unconditional love permeates every teddy bear and angel. I can almost see you under the pink quilt.

I love to talk with you just as I did before you transitioned into your new life. I still can hear you, even though you did not speak. Every moment in your presence is profound and meaningful. I am simultaneously filled with love and sorrow. Bittersweet.

I stand here open hearted, transparent, vulnerable, fragile, and resilient. I am all that you taught me to be, and I share your life and love.

- Who is your teacher? Let them know what they have taught you.

Bittersweet Gratitude

December 19th

"It is the nature of grace to fill spaces that have been empty."
- Goethe

In experiencing the loss of my beloved daughter Ashley, I find so many open spaces in my life. Open and empty spaces where I would call to her, "Good morning sweetheart, how do you feel this morning?" Say goodnight with a prayer of gratitude and a kiss on her forehead. Those and many other moments are now open.

Now what do I do? Well, Ashley still speaks to me. "Tell my story Daddy. Help others who have special needs children. Share my lessons of resilience and unconditional love."

This is my bittersweet gratitude. Even though she is not physically here she sends blessings. This inheritance of giving to someone else, what she has given to me. I hear her voice. I am surrounded by her pictures. I am lifted up in her unconditional love. I share her unconditional, universal love and she is forever alive.

♦ Reflect on this quote from *Bittersweet: How Sorrow and Longing Make Us Whole* by Susan Cain, "The place you suffer…is the same place you care profoundly-care enough to act."

Letting Go

December 20th

At this time in my life, I am learning to let go, again. In the past few years, I have let go of some dreams, I have faced open-heart surgery, and I have been at my precious daughter's bedside as she passed from this life. All terrible letting go experiences.

Each time I needed to let go, I needed to believe in something holding me, comforting me, loving me. I have come to believe that presence, that unconditional love, is God. As my fear dissipates, as my grief becomes less immobilizing, I gradually open up.

All that I love, all that I am is in God's hands.

I have come to experience that even in moments of sheer terror and unceasing grief, there is a light. Similar to the eye of a hurricane. In its center, pure calm. When I was wheeled into heart surgery, at the core of my fear was the knowing that I was in God's hands, and whatever the outcome, all would be well. When I kissed my little girl's forehead for the last time and told her I loved her and thanked her for being with us for 39 years, even then, even now, as I weep writing these words, I know she was in God's loving embrace and somehow, even though I don't know how all would be well.

Each time I let go, I learn and re-learn God's unconditional love is always with me.

◆ In quiet meditation, consciously breathe in unconditional love and notice how the stress in your body decreases.

"Heaven on Earth is a Choice You Make, Not a Place You Find."
~ Wayne Dyer

December 21st

Every day, every moment is an opportunity. Will we choose love or fear? Will we choose heaven or hell? When we choose love, we choose heaven where we fully commit to life.

Every time we let those we love know that we love them, every time we reflect on our own journey and realize we are better today than we were yesterday, in all of these moments, we are creating heaven on earth.

"The Kingdom of God is within you."
- Luke 17:21, *The Holy Bible, New King James Version*

Everyday life and love are calling us to embrace life. Embrace love. Embrace each other. Heaven is in the embrace.

- Please share a long embrace with a dear friend or loved one.

How Do We Find Our Deepest and Best Self?

December 22nd

Throughout my life, I have found that some of the important tools and practices are prayer, meditation, service to others, art, poetry, solitude, nature, music, empathy, compassion, trust, truth, and love.

Always love.

I find it is always important to accept life as it impacts us. What we resist, will persist. Acceptance of the pandemic or acceptance of my heart surgery means I do my part. I wear my mask and get my vaccinations. I get my heart surgery and follow my plant-based diet and continue my exercise program.

The essence of life is that we are loved, unconditionally loved by a Divinity that is with us and in us. I rejoice in every experience life has given me… the laughter and the tears.

Love is in every moment.

- What are your most important practices for your deepest and best self?
- What do you rejoice in?

I've Been Broken Open

December 23rd

I've been broken open. I have embraced my vulnerability. The morning light that bleaches the dogwood tree, the bluebird that flits across my vision, the chipmunk that scampers up the tree, the rain that drops liquid pebbles in our pond.

I am human, frail, faltering, resilient, and compassionate. I listen for the Divine harmony in all of life.

Every moment is a sacred opportunity. Every breath is amazing. Let us embrace the exquisite vulnerability of life.

♦ With a trusted friend, share a time in your life when you were broken open. Share the challenges and pleasures of this experience.

Hard Wired for Connection

December 24th

Let us all acknowledge that we need each other. We are "hardwired for connection" says Brené Brown. We thrive on connection and belonging. Let us open our hearts and minds to the love that is being given to us and give our love unceasingly.

We are social beings. We need to feel connection, empathy, compassion, and physical touch. These past few years of the pandemic have increased our fear and isolation. We have adapted to connect through technology, but we missed the physical closeness. We miss the facial expressions and human touch.

We are each and emanation of Divine love. We each can share the warmth of spirit with everyone we meet. Open your heart, open your mind, open your arms, and connect with a fellow human.

- With a trusted friend, share your experience of isolation and need for connection. Allow yourself to be aware of the feeling of warmth when you hold each other's hands or hug.

Every Moment is Sacred

December 25th

In this Christmas season, allow yourself to remember that every moment is sacred. In every moment, the sacredness of life is being expressed. Somewhere flowers bloom. Somewhere a bee is gathering pollen and somewhere a bird is singing its life. In your life, children have been born and loved ones have passed. In this life, a smile can lift your heart and someone's tears can touch your soul.

Let us all remember the sacred moments of laughter, deep conversation, meaningful connection, and unconditional love. We have all overcome challenges, and it is time to hold hands, heal hearts, and come together.

- In quiet reflection, focus on the challenges you have experienced this past year.
- What lessons have you learned and how have you become a better person through these experiences?

Home

December 26th

In the depths of our heart, we long for intimacy with unconditional love with the Divine. The tug we feel is Divinity beckoning us home. The paradox is that heaven (our home) is hidden in our hearts. We long for what we already have. The homesickness we feel can be resolved with quiet, silent mindfulness. In stillness, you will find your way home.

- In quiet reflection, focus on unconditional love. Breathe in love and consciously breathe out love. Repeat this process at least three times.

A Meditation on Gratitude

December 27th

Sit quietly. Let the presence of unconditional love fill your heart and mind. Allow yourself to be filled with gratitude. Remember all the good, all the blessings that have been poured into your life.

You are not alone. Nothing can separate you from God's love. Be grateful for God's love. Be grateful for your family, your friends, your life.

As you move through your day, look for the treasures of spirit that have been left for you to find. Retrieve these gifts and hold them close. At the end of your day's journey, you will have a treasure chest of love.

Offer your thanks with a grateful heart. May love and peace guide you to sleep with grateful thoughts playing a lullaby in your mind.

♦ Reflect on a person who needs your gratitude. Hold that person in your mind and send thoughts of gratitude to them.

As Educators…

December 28th

"A man has made at least a start on discovering the meaning of human life when he plants shade trees under which he knows full well he will never sit."
- Elton Trueblood, *The Life We Prize*

As educators this quote sums up our life of commitment to our students. As educators our life is service and legacy. We serve through dedication, detail, inspiration, motivation, tough love, discipline, forgiveness, compassion, empathy, and creativity. Our legacy is formed in every student who believes in themselves, learns to work with others, finds their purpose, serves their country and community, and who leaves the world a bit better because their teacher modeled that for them.

"The seed never sees the flower."
- Zen Proverb

As educators, we are seed planters. We plant seed after seed, believing in the process of life and education. We practice a faith as deep as nature itself. Every action, every word, every lesson has a ripple effect; even generations after us. Every student we impact affects the world and all its people.

As educators we play a significant role in the health and healing of the world.

Everything we do matters to someone.

- What have you planted today?

Sharing Fears to Heal

December 29th

"What we hold dear can heal the world."
- Mark Nepo

I have learned that what we fear to share, our deepest feelings, connects us to everyone. When we share our feelings, and especially our fears, we give others the permission to be vulnerable, transparent, and courageous.

When we release our fears and witness others releasing their fears, we create a healing bond.

- How are you giving yourself permission to be vulnerable, transparent, and courageous?

Claim the Gift

December 30th

I am your friend. My love, respect, and appreciation for you goes deep. Although I have attempted to give you all that I have, I am aware there is nothing I can give which you do not already possess. There is very much, however, that you can claim. The peace of heaven can come to us when we find peace in the smallest gift in our day. Claim the peace.

The negativity and judgment of the world is a shadow. Behind the shadow, within our reach, is joy. In every challenge, there is a gift. Claim the gift.

Life gives abundantly. We judge the gifts and ignore or cast them away. Open the gift, rejoice in the splendor woven by God's love, wisdom, and power.

Claim it, grasp it, and you touch the Holy Spirit that brings it to you. Everything we call a trial, sorrow or duty, spirit's hand is still there.

Life is bursting with meaning and purpose- full of beauty. What we refer to as a reality, cloaks the true reality…the reality of heaven on Earth.

Draw on courage to claim it is all that is required. Courage is your spiritual birthright. We are all together, finding our way home.

So, at this moment, I greet you. I acknowledge you, not quite as the world greets you, but with profound esteem, respect, and love. I greet you now and forever as the day breaks and the first light of morning sends rays of spirit to banish the night.

- Claim your gift now!

A New Day is Rising

December 31st

I see the Divine in the flowers, trees, and bird song. I see the Divine in you and sometimes me. I strive to see the beauty of creation in everything and everyone. There is a grace, a blessing, and unconditional loving presence above, below, and within all things and all life.

I believe this unconditional loving presence is so abundant it cannot be imprisoned by hate and greed. The presence of love seeps through.

I rejoice in the unconditional love that always finds a way to comfort and heal. When we are at our last breath, this loving power is there to keep us from drowning.

We are the emanations of this love. We are here for a purpose. We must share the light and love of spirit.

Sing a song of gratitude. Let your joy for life shine. Know that unconditional love will always negate the darkness.

A new day is rising.

- Celebrate a new day rising with loved ones and friends. Share your song of gratitude.

Notes

January

4 January 2nd - *A Course of Miracles* by Helen Schucman and William Thetford (1976)

6 January 4th - *The Book of Joy* by His Holiness the Dalai Lama and Archbishop Desmond Tutu, (2016)

7 January 5th - *The Rabbit Effect: Live Longer, Happier, and Healthier with the Groundbreaking Science of Kindness* by Dr. Kelli Harding (2019)

11 January 9th - *Building Academic Success: A Resource Guide for Enhancing Higher Education Outcomes* by Michael Theall and Jennifer R. Keup (2004)

12 January 10th - *The Courage to Teach: Exploring the Inner Landscape of a Teacher's Life* by Parker Palmer (1997)

20 January 17th - *Finnish Lessons: What Can the World Learn from Educational Change in Finland?* by Pasi Sahlberg (2011)

26 January 22nd - *Wishful Thinking: A Theological ABC* by Frederick Buechner (1973)

34 January 30th - *The Book of Awakening: Having the Life You Want by Being Present to the Life You Have* by Mark Nepo (2000)

February

36 February - "Auguries of Innocence" by William Blake (1863)

37 February 1st - *Daring Greatly: How the Courage to Be Vulnerable Transforms the Way We Live, Love, Parent, and Lead* by Dr. Brené Brown (2012)

40 February 4th - *The Book of Awakening: Having the Life You Want by Being Present to the Life You Have* by Mark Nepo (2000)

44 February 7th - *Awakening Imagination* by Neville Goddard (1952)

46 February 9th - *Pensées* by Blaise Pascal (1670)

50 February 13th - *Thoughts in Solitude* by Thomas Merton (1956)

50 February 13th - *The Gospel of Thomas: The Hidden Sayings of Jesus* by Marvin Meyer (1992)

54 February 17th - "Lines Written a Few Miles Above Tintern Abbey, on Revisiting the Banks of the Wye during a Tour, July 13, 1798" by William Wordsworth (1798)

55 February 18th - *Wanted: Hero* by Jaime Buckley (2013)

56 February 19th - *No Death, No Fear* by Thich Nhãt Hahn (2002)

59 February 22nd - *Power vs. Force: The Hidden Determinants of Human Behavior* by Dr. David Hawkins (1995)

60 February 23rd - *The Prophet* by Kahlil Gibran (1923)

63 February 26th - *A Book of Psalms: Selected and Adapted from the Hebrew* by Stephen Mitchell (1994)

64 February 27th - *The Holy Bible, English Standard Version,* John 14:20 (2001)

66 February 29th - *The Book of Awakening: Having the Life You Want by Being Present to the Life You Have* by Mark Nepo (2000)

March

68 March - *Man's Search for Meaning* by Viktor E. Frankl (1946)

75 March 7th - *The Rabbit Effect: Live Longer, Happier, and Healthier with the Groundbreaking Science of Kindness* by Dr. Kelli Harding (2019)

77 March 8th - *Winnie-the-Pooh* by A.A. Milne (1926)

84 March 15th - *Leaves of Grass* by Walt Whitman (1855)

86 March 17th - *Daring Greatly: How the Courage to Be Vulnerable Transforms the Way We Live, Love, Parent, and Lead* by Dr. Brené Brown (2012)

88 March 19th - *Doctrine of the Mean (Zhongyong)* by Confucius

88 March 19th - *The Book of Awakening: Having the Life You Want by Being Present to the Life You Have* by Mark Nepo (2000)

88 March 19th - "Anthem" from *The Future* by Leonard Cohen (1992)

96 March 27th - *Strength to Love* by Reverend Dr. Martin Luther King Jr. (1963)

100 March 30th - *Life 101: Everything We Wish We Had Learned About Life in School—But Didn't* by Peter McWilliams (1990)

April

111 April 9th - *The Game of Life and How to Play It* by Florence Scovel Shinn (1925)

113 April 11th - *Cultivating Gratitude in the Classroom* by Sarah McKibben (2013)

117 April 14th - “The Rose” from *Growing Up in Hollywood Town* written by Amanda McBroom (1980)

120 April 16th - *Thus Spoke Zarathustra* by Friedrich Nietzsche (1885)

124 April 20th - *Words Can Change Your Brain: 12 Conversation Strategies to Build Trust, Resolve Conflict, and Increase Intimacy* by Dr. Andrew Newberg and Mark Waldman (2012)

129 April 25th - *The Holy Bible, New King James Version,* Philippians 4:8 (1982)

May

136 May - *Handbook to Higher Consciousness* by Ken Keyes, Jr. (1975)

137 May 1st - *The Heart of Higher Education: A Call to Renewal* by Parker Palmer, Arthur Zajonc, and Megan Scribner (2010)

139 May 3rd - *Leadership in Turbulent Times* by Kearns Goodwin (2018)

145 May 8th - *The Rabbit Effect: Live Longer, Happier, and Healthier with the Groundbreaking Science of Kindness* by Dr. Kelli Harding (2019)

148 May 10th - *Preventing adolescent health-risk behaviors by strengthening protection during childhood* by Hawkins, J. D., Catalano, R. F., Kosterman, R., Abbott, R., & Hill, K. G. (1999)

148 May 10th - *Children's social behaviors as predictors of academic achievement: A longitudinal analysis* by Malecki, C. K., & Elliott, S. N. (2002)

149 May 11th - *State of America's Children 2023* by Children's Defense Fund (2023)

152 May 13th - *Les Misérables* by Victor Hugo (1862)

154 May 15th - *The Prophet* by Kahlil Gibran (1923)

156 May 17th - *The Book of Awakening: Having the Life You Want by Being Present to the Life You Have* by Mark Nepo (2000)

157 May 18th - *The Holy Bible, English Standard Version,* Luke 23:34 (2001)

160 May 20th - *The Impossible Will Take a Little While: Perseverance and Hope in Troubled Times* by Paul Rogat Loeb (2004)

162 May 22nd - *The Circle of the Way: A Concise History of Zen from the Buddha to the Modern World* by Barbara O'Brien (2019)

163 May 23rd - *The Age of Empathy: Nature's Lessons for a Kinder Society* by Frans de Waal (2019)

173 May 31st - *Resilience from the Heart: The Power to Thrive in Life's Extremes* by Gregg Braden (2015)

June

175 June 1st - *The Power of You: 365 Daily Reflections* by Chris Michaels (2015)

177 June 3rd - *The 7 Habits of Highly Effective People* by Stephen R. Covey (1989)

181 June 7th - *The Book of Awakening: Having the Life You Want by Being Present to the Life You Have* by Mark Nepo (2000)

181 June 7th - *The Hero with a Thousand Faces* by Joseph Campbell (1949)

182 June 8th - *The Fire Next Time* by James Baldwin (1963)

202 June 28th - *Into the Magic Shop: A Neurosurgeon's Quest to Discover the Mysteries of the Brain and the Secrets of the Heart by* Dr. James Doty (2016)

204 June 30th - *The Places That Scare You: A Guide to Fearlessness in Difficult Times* by Pema Chödrön (2001)

July

205 July and August - *Daring Greatly: How the Courage to Be Vulnerable Transforms the Way We Live, Love, Parent, and Lead* by Dr. Brené Brown (2012)

209 July 3rd - *No Man Is an Island* by Thomas Merton (1955)

213 July 7th - *The Trust Factor: The Science of Creating High-Performance Companies* by Dr. Paul Zak (2017)

214 July 7th - *Self-Compassion: The Proven Power of Being Kind to Yourself* by Dr. Kristin Neff (2011)

216 July 9th - *Attachment and Loss, Volume 1: Attachment* by John Bowlby (1969)

217 July 10th - *The Rabbit Effect: Live Longer, Happier, and Healthier with the Groundbreaking Science of Kindness* by Dr. Kelli Harding (2019)

218 July 11th - *Interpreting Darwin* by Leon C. Megginson (1992)

224 July 17th - “Pogo”, created by Walt Kelly (1971)

224 July 17th - *The Holy Bible, New King James Version,* 1 Peter 2:17 (1982)

226 July 19th - *The Art of Loving* by Erich Fromm (1956)

229 July 22nd - *The Five Side Effects of Kindness: This Book Will Make You Feel Better, Be Happier & Live Longer* by Dr. David Hamilton (2017)

237 July 30th - *The Talmud, The William Davidson Edition* (2023)

224 July 31st - *The Inner Path from Where You Are to Where You Want to Be* by Terry Cole-Whittaker (1986)

August

241 August 2nd - "Spring Cleaning", *Joan of Arcadia*, Season 2, Episode 14 (2005)

248 August 9th - *The World According to Mister Rogers: Important Things to Remember* by Fred Rogers (2003)

258 August 18th - *Empathy: Why It Matters, and How to Get It* by Roman Krznaric (2014)

258 August 18th - *Daring Greatly: How the Courage to Be Vulnerable Transforms the Way We Live, Love, Parent, and Lead* by Dr. Brené Brown (2012)

264 August 23rd - *Letters to a Young Poet* by Rainer Maria Rilke (1929)

268 August 27th - *The Book of Awakening: Having the Life You Want by Being Present to the Life You Have* by Mark Nepo (2000)

271 August 30th - *The Principles of Psychology* by William James (1890)

September

304 September 27th - *The Book of Awakening: Having the Life You Want by Being Present to the Life You Have* by Mark Nepo (2000)
306 September 29th - *Forgive and Forget: Healing the Hurts We Don't Deserve* by Lewis B. Smedes (1984)
307 September 30th - *Finding Inner Courage* by Mark Nepo (2007)

October

310 October 1st - “Christus Vivit: Post-Synodal Apostolic Exhortation” by Pope Francis (2019)
311 October 2nd - *All About Love: New Visions* by bell hooks (2000)
311 October 2nd - *The Book of Forgiving: The Fourfold Path for Healing Ourselves and Our World* by Archbishop Desmond Tutu and Mpho Tutu (2014)
314 October 5th - *The Book of Awakening: Having the Life You Want by Being Present to the Life You Hav*e by Mark Nepo (2000)
321 October 12th - "The Road Not Taken" by Robert Frost (1916)
329 October 20th - *Illusions: The Adventures of a Reluctant Messiah* by Richard Bach (1977)
332 October 23rd - “A World Split Apart” by Alexander Solzhenitsyn (1978)

November

345 November 3rd - *The Gospel of Thomas: The Hidden Sayings of Jesus* by Marvin Meyer (1992)
351 November 9th - *The Holy Bible, English Standard Version,* Romans 12:2 (2001)
361 November 19th - *The Power of Myth* by Joseph Campbell (1988)

363 November 21st - *Illusions: The Adventures of a Reluctant Messiah* by Richard Bach (1977)
365 November 23rd - "First Inaugural Address" by Abraham Lincoln (1861)
366 November 24th - *Devotions upon Emergent Occasions* by John Donne (1624)
369 November 27th - *The Holy Bible, King James Version,* Matthew 12:31 (1611)
371 November 29th - "The Hill We Climb" by Amanda Gorman (2021)
372 November 30th - *The World According to Mister Rogers: Important Things to Remember* by Fred Rogers (2003)

December

375 December 2nd - *The Holy Bible, New King James Version,* Ephesians 4:6 (1982)
378 December 5th - "Desiderata" by Max Ehrmann (1927)
388 December 15th - *Gift from the Sea* by Anne Morrow Lindbergh (1955)
390 December 17th - *You Can Heal Your Life* by Louise Hay (1984)
392 December 19th - *Bittersweet: How Sorrow and Longing Make Us Whole* by Susan Cain (2022)
394 December 21st - *The Holy Bible, New King James Version,* Luke 17:21 (1982)
401 December 28th - *The Life We Prize* by Elton Trueblood (1983)